Metamorphosed Skill and Talent: An Inclusive Critique of India

Author: Col Ashwani Kumar Joshi (Retd), Ph.D.

Co- Authors: Abha Joshi & Medha Pandey

ZORBA BOOKS

ZORBA BOOKS

Published by Zorba Books, September 2023
Website: www.zorbabooks.com
Email: info@zorbabooks.com
Author Name & Copyright © Dr. Ashwani Kumar Joshi
Title: Metamorphosed Skill and Talent: An Inclusive Critique of India

Printbook ISBN: 978-93-5896-005-1
Ebook ISBN: 978-93-5896-006-8

Zorba Books Pvt. Ltd. (opc)
Sushant Arcade,
Next to Courtyard Marriot,
Sushant Lok 1, Gurgaon – 122009, India

List of Tables

List of Figures

List of Abbreviations

AICTE:	All India Council for Technical Education
AIU:	Association of Indian Universities
BFSI:	Banking, Financial Services and Insurance
BPO:	Business Process Outsourcing
CACs:	Common Assessment Centres
CFA:	Confirmatory Factor Analysis
CII:	Confederation of Indian Industry
CSCM:	Centrally Sponsored Centrally Managed (CSCM)
CSSM:	Centrally Sponsored State Managed (CSSM)
CL:	Confidence level
COE:	Centre of Excellence
DSC:	District Skill Committee
EFA:	Exploratory Factor Analysis
EY:	Ernst & Young
FICCI:	Federation of Indian Chambers of Commerce and Industry
GoI:	Government of India
IOCL:	Indian Oil Corporation Limited

IT:	Information Technology
ITeS:	Information Technology Enabled Services
KPO:	Knowledge Process Outsourcing
MSDE:	Ministry of Skill Development and Entrepreneurship
NCAER:	National Council of Applied Economic Research
NCVET:	National Council of Vocational Education and Training
NSDC:	National Skill Development Corporation
NSQF:	National Skill Qualification Framework
OECD:	Organisation for Economic Corporation and Development
PMKVY:	Pradhan Mantri Kaushal Vikas Yojana
PPP:	Public Private Partnership
PwC:	PricewaterCoopers
RPL:	Recognition of Prior Learning
SANKALP:	Skills Acquisition and Knowledge Awareness for Livelihood Promotion
SME:	Small to Medium Enterprise
SSC:	Sector Skill Council
SSDM:	State Skill Development Mission
STAR:	National Skill Certification and Reward Scheme
STEM:	Science, Technology, Engineering and Mathematics
STRIVE:	Skill Strengthening for Industrial Value Enhancement
STT:	Short Term Training
SURYA:	Skilling, Up-skilling, Re-skilling of Youth and Assessment

TITP:	Technical Intern Training Program
ToT:	Training of Trainer
TP:	Training Partner
UIDAI:	Unique Identification Authority of India
UNDP:	United Nations Development Program
UNICEF:	United Nations International Children's Emergency Fund
UTs:	Union Territories
WISE:	World Indicators of Skills for Employment

Contents

Abstract

India enjoys 'Demographic Dividend' which is at its peak presently, with its youth's median age of 29 years and is likely to last till 2040. The working age population between 15-59 yrs. is about 62%. During next 20 yrs. the global workforce is going to decline by 4 % while India will increase by 32%. About 10% of the work force has undergone formal and informal training in India as against over 95% in South Korea and over 51% in U.S.A. It gives India a majestic opportunity in becoming a major supplier of the skilled workforce globally. This will also solve the crisis of employability and widespread poverty.

With the above in mind, Pradhan Mantri Kaushal Vikas Yojana (PMKVY) was launched in July 2015 . It was followed by PMKVY 2.0 which aimed at skilling 10 million youth between 2016-2020. Recently, in January, 2021, PMKVY 3.0 was launched with has a target to skilling eight lacs youth in the FY 2020-21. Orders regarding Constitution of Steering Committee for PMKVY 4.0 and Executive Committee for Skill Hub for implementation of PMKVY 4.0 have been issued. However, approval of the PMKVY 4.0 by the cabinet is awaited.

No empirical research has been done to study the effectiveness of the PMKVY. For this purpose, the state of Haryana has been chosen for 'A Study of the Effectiveness of Pradhan Mantri Kaushal Vikas Yojana in select Districts of Haryana'.

Acknowledgement

First and foremost, my sincere gratitude to the God Almighty who gave me an opportunity to write this book.

I am also highly indebted to Prof. A.R. Dubey, Vice Chancellor, Lingaya's Vidyapeeth, Faridabad and Prof. Sandeep Singh Chib for their guidance. I would especially want to thank Haryana Skill Development mission for allowing the survey of trainees participating in the Pradhan Mantri Kaushal Vikas Yojana.

I am profoundly grateful to my parents for their blessings to accomplish this work. Many thanks to my wife, Ms. Abha Joshi and my children for the unconditional support, encouragement and the time that I should have been given to them.

Ashwani Kumar Joshi

Preface

It lends credence when an impact assessment of a policy and the strategies are undertaken together. Such an exercise bolsters efforts on the counts of advocacy, analysis , accountability and allocation of the resources.

This book is an attempt to assess the efficacy of the Skill Development Scheme of Prime minister, popularly known as Pradhan Mantri Kaushal Vikas Yojana (PMKVY).

The authors have examined the PMKVY in all its facets and aspects only to underscore the importance of such a scheme for providing the tools and drivers to the unemployed youth of the country for their livelihood. An inclusive case study of Haryana has brought to the fore, the odyssey, oasis and practicality embedded in the Mission and Vision of PMKVY in an illustrious and style of those of the connoisseurs. It is hoped that this will be useful and render an invaluable insight to the readers in particular, and; to the stakeholders of PMKVY in general.

This systematic empirical study maybe epoch making in the domain which sets the sails for reaching the 'highly skilled' level from unskilled beginning. The lessons learnt by Haryana in consonance with PMKVY can be emulated by various geographies not only in India but in any part of the world.

Foreword

Pradhan Mantri Kaushal Vikas Yojana (PMKVY) was launched in 2015 to provide outcome-based skilling based on the industry validated standards. On successful completion of the skilling, the trainees were given a government recognised certificate, financial reward and facilitation for employment. The overarching objective was to harness demographic dividend, bridge the gap between demand and supply of the skilled workforce , help in sustainable livelihood to the youth and alleviate poverty.

The Ministry of Skill Development and Entrepreneurship had created in November 2014 under a cabinet minister, gave impetus to the skill development through coordinated efforts, laying out common norms, building capacity of vocational and technical training framework, building new skills, endeavour to make skills aspirational and work together with Ministry of HRD to encourage vocational education in academic institutes

Such an endeavour has given the Skill Development of unemployed youth, a seat on the table. There are currently thirty-six sector skill councils in India and the industry representatives as members of the Governing Bodies of these sector skill councils.

It is so far so good but the effectiveness of this mammoth herculean task needs the resources, especially; the time for acquiring the skills that are needed in the industries and markets in a nation.

Though the new fillip and impetus have been accorded to PMKVY, it needs be evaluated whether it serves the populace for which the Honourable Prime Minister had devised this scheme. This book is an attempt in this direction.

The authors have made a sincere effort by focusing on the state of Haryana. Probably, the impact assessment has used the inverted pyramid method of PMKVY, the evolutionary method and also the theme-based study for completing the cycle to conceptualise, identify the principle on which it is based and to theorize the flow.

Undoubtedly, this book has used the triangulation method to study PMKVY in totality. It is crystal clear that the authors have delineated the context and conditions, the tasks which the skilled personnel are expected to accomplish, the evidences of the efficacy of imparting the training, the criteria for competency judgement besides the administrative paraphernalia needed for such an endeavour.

Though this study was completed by the end of 2021; an *epilogue* has been provided towards the end of this book so that the readers may glean the updated information.

At this juncture, it has become imperative on the readers to take into account; the facts that India is the most populated country in the world and thus it possesses the 'highest number of young people' bubbling with energy , self-motivation of highest order and they are ready to take India to the world by using their skill, knowledge, synergy at the place where India is numero uno country.

Though the zenith and summit are elusive as of now, the projections and the cues are indicating that demographic dividend of India will be there by 2040. This assumption is based on the parameters of the human sustenance index, per capita income, GDP of India and the glaring context of India becoming the fourth largest economy poised to be number THREE shortly which is not a mean achievement.

This book has been organised in the format i.e., Introduction, the context, Methodologies Used for Collection of Data and the Related Analysis, Processual Delivery of Training, Outcome of the Study, Conclusion and; lastly, the Epilogue.

The details of the Case are permeating throughout this book, the use of case Study research method notwithstanding.

This work does not claim to be the first of its kind but it is certainly the very first study, so far as the impact assessment of PMKVY is concerned.

The diction, the repertoire, the lucidity and even the innovative study are pervading throughout this book and it is hoped earnestly that the readers will offer their insight, comments and critique for making this book better when its second edition hits the stalls and other online marketing platforms.

Chapter 1

Introduction

1.1 Introduction

This chapter provides an overview of the study, leading to the research study's problem statement and reasoning. It also presents a brief critique on the Pradhan Mantri Kaushal Vikas Yojana, PMKVY which is the core of the study and further setting the grounds for case selection as Haryana to evaluate its efficacy, therein, from the trainees/youth beneficiary's perspective. This chapter also enumerates the objectives of the study along with a brief description of the research approach. All this will set the basic foundation for the study. Subsequently the chapter concludes with the significance of the study and the outline of the thesis.

1.2 Overview of the Study

In recent years, India's economy has risen to become one of the world's fastest expanding, mainly due to its 'Demographic dividend', which is currently at its pinnacle, with a median age of 29 years among its youth. According to the United Nations Population Fund (UNFPA) Demographic dividend, is "the economic growth potential that can result from shifts in population's age structure, primarily when the share of working age population (15-64) is greater than the share of non-working age population (14 and younger and 65 and older).". India's demographic dividend started in 1980 and is likely to end in 2040. This implies that India will experience an age advantage for at least two decades, through 2040. It has the potential to become a major worldwide supply of personnel if its youth are properly trained. This will also solve the crisis of employability and poverty, and also raise the youth productivity, thereby leading to sustainable development of the nation. As a result, youth development is critical. 'Skilling' refers to training in practical, theoretical, and soft skills in accordance with industrial standards. This means training the youth to make them 'employable' and self-sufficient to earn a sustainable livelihood.

Many studies, however, have confirmed the existence of a 'Skill-Gap' in the Indian economy. To meet the demands of a burgeoning population, India would need roughly 400 million skilled individuals by 2022. However, the youth's current level of readiness to meet this need is insufficient. First, in comparison to other countries, India has a very low supply of skilled workers (10 percent, including 4% who have received formal training and 6% who have received informal training). For example, China has a skilled workforce of 47 percent, Germany has a skilled workforce of 74 percent, and Korea has a skilled workforce of 96 percent. Second, the level of competence and training, or 'employability,' of young people who have completed technical training or higher education in accordance with industry needs is modest. To put it another way, according to the India Skills Report 2019, technical graduates' employability was 63.11 percent, while MBA and polytechnic graduates' employability was 47.18 percent and 45.90 percent, respectively. Third, the demand-supply imbalance is expanding as a result of a shortage of training opportunities and young mobilisation to participate in such training on cutting-edge technologies and sectors.

The Indian government along with the state and local government interface is working hard to achieve the objective set and has a positive impact on youth. The different bodies in the skilling ecosystem in India are presented in the figure 1 below: -

Figure 1.1: Skilling ecosystem in India, Unlocking the potential of youth

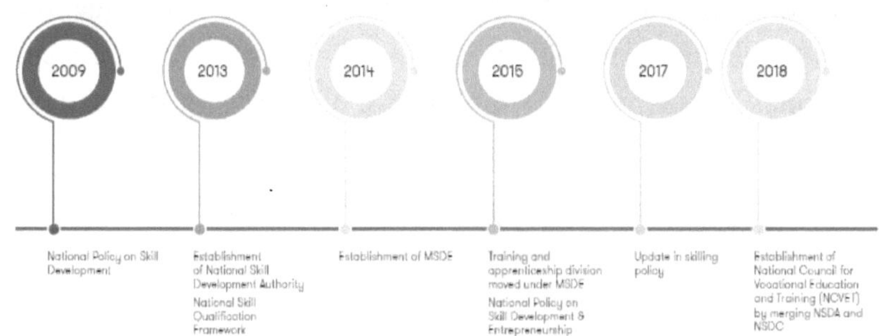

Source: https://www.grantthornton.in/globalassets/1.-member-firms/india/assets/pdfs/skilling-ecosystem-in-india-unlocking-the-potential-of-youth.pdf

The skilling ecosystem is constrained to an extent with certain problems and challenges that need to be resolved.

In the first place, to make the workforce employable, it is necessary to skill/reskill them. (Skilled implies acquiring the ability and capacity to carry out complicated activities or job functions involving cognitive abilities, technical abilities, and/or people in a seamless and adaptive manner through purposeful, methodical, and consistent effort (interpersonal skills).

Second, the delivery mechanism for skills is not standardized. Besides the Ministry of Skill Development and Entrepreneurship (MSDE), 17 other ministries also hire qualified candidates. Following common norms for skilling is a challenge in itself.

Third, the data of the skilled workforce is inadequate. Thus, connecting employers to the job seeker is yet to be optimized. Moreover, the youth is not employable as skill sets required by the industry are missing.

Fourth, the skilling effort across 17 ministries and states is fragmented. Integrated delivery framework is missing. Common norms are not followed.

Fifth, access i.e., reaching the unreachable and disadvantaged is not there. The informal sector employs 93 percent of the workers, posing a significant problem.

Sixth, has been observed that youths are often trained in one occupational position and then play another. People have been tested and qualified for a specific employment role in the past, only to wind up in an entirely different one. Furthermore, training is not aligned with demand, which means that we train a lot of people for some jobs that aren't in high demand. To enable youth's employability and sustainable livelihood, these sectors must be addressed in the skill ecosystem.

In order to skill and empower the youth, our Honorable Prime Minister Shri Narendra Modi ji launched a Skill India campaign on 15 July, 2015 on the occasion of World Youth Skills Day

By 2022, the goal is to train over 40 crore individuals in various skills across India. The following are some of the initiatives that are part of this campaign:

- National Skill Development Mission
- National Policy for Skill Development and Entrepreneurship, 2015
- Pradhan Mantri Kaushal Vikas Yojana (PMKVY)
- Skill Loan scheme

❖ *The MSDE's Pradhan Mantri Kaushal Vikas Yojana (PMKVY)* is a result-based skill training programme that strives to provide youth with meaningful, industry-relevant, and skill-based training. The goal of this skill certification and reward system is to enable and motivate a large number of Indian youths to pursue skill training, find work, and earn a living. On successful completion of the programme, the participants were given a government certification and a monetary prize, which will help them make money. As a result, the PMKVY was created as a key measure to provide youth with skill-based training, allowing them to earn and contribute to anti-poverty efforts by establishing a sustainable livelihood

❖ So, this study is devoted to unraveling the PMKVY 2.0 as specifically implemented in select districts of Haryana.

1.3 Problem Statement

As discussed above, the Pradhan Mantri Kaushal Vikas Yojana (PMKVY) is an outcome-based skill training program by the MSDE that aims to offer meaningful, industry relevant, and skill-based training to the youth. The purpose of this skill certification and reward system is to allow and mobilise the majority of the Indian youth to take up skill training and become employable and earn a living. However, in the context of the PMKVY, reports and studies have pointed out that there are many skilling challenges that pertain to the scale, speed and standard under PMKVY that is not up to the desired level. Some of the reasons are paucity of certified trainers, assessors, quality infrastructure, participation by the industry and funding (public and private). The youth is not inspired to undergo skills training under PMKVY due to the aspiration of vocational training visa via acquiring education qualifications, poor job placement and skill premium in the salaries. Inadequate emphasis on the cognitive and soft skills, focus on the STEM requirement, skilling the trainees as per the international standards to enable international mobility are certain important areas that need attention. The major challenges are in inadequate industry participation, monitoring & evaluation, placements/jobs, skills for future and limited studies on impact analysis.

In this backdrop, this study intends to critically analyze the PMKVY as implemented in the districts of Haryana to:

- Determine whether the youth have been appropriately empowered and mobilized to participate in the skills training.
- How training is imparted to them in terms of quality of the trainers, training facility/infrastructure, training material, equipment and resources and counseling/mentoring and placement support services,
- Understand the outcome benefits of the PMKVY training,
- Examine the impact of PMKVY training on youth/beneficiary, whether they are enabled to attain gainful employment to earn a decent living or not.

The study was carried out to better understand the training program's procedure and to evaluate the PMKVY training's effectiveness in terms of skill enhancement, satisfaction and standard of living, chalk out and suggest ways for the improvement of the PMKVY training program and implementation in different regions. Thus, the scope of the study extends to examining in-depth the PMKVY training and its efficacy from the youth's perspective in select districts of Haryana. In the light of this, it will recommend the ways for improvement and measures to plug in the gaps/deficiencies in the PMKVY training planning and implementation that can be extended to other geographical locations in the country.

1.4 Rationale of the Study

PMKVY is perceived to play a pivotal role in skilling and thus enhancing youth's employability in a large way. This is evinced in the extant review studies and reports. In this context, it has concentrated on the importance of skilling, skilling interventions, description of the various skilling indicators (skill acquisition, skill prerequisites, skill mismatch, and economic and societal outcomes are all aspects to consider.), contribution of skill development in achieving sustainable and inclusive growth, skill development initiatives, status of vocational education & training ecosystem and the impact of the skill India training programme on young people. But there is hardly any empirical research study focused on the PMKVY as perceived by the trainees/beneficiaries (youth). In the last about six years of inception of the PMKVY, it is critical to assess PMKVY's role and effects. So, it is pertinent to conduct an empirical study concentrating on the PMKVY's role, influence and its perception by the youth in select districts in Haryana.

1.5 Background of the Skill Development Initiatives by the GoI

The government launched the National Skill Certification and Reward Scheme (STAR) in 2013, funding Rs 1000 crores to train 10 million youths. Globally many countries were aging while India had the demographic dividend. Only about 10 percent of the workforce had undergone vocational training (4 percent formal training and balance informal). Acknowledging the skilling challenge, NSDC was formed in 2008 and MSDE of Skill Development & in 2014. On World Youth Day, July 15, 2015, Prime Minister Narendra Modi formally inaugurated the Skill India Mission, unveiling the new "National Policy for Skill Development and Entrepreneurship 2015" as well as the Ministry's flagship initiative, Pradhan Mantri Kaushal Vikas Yojana (PMKVY).

The Ministry of Labor's training and apprenticeship programmes were handed to MSDE. PMKVY was approved by the government on March 20, 2015, with a budget of Rs 1500 crores with the goal of training 24 lakh people (14 lakh fresh trainees and 10 lakh RPL). The NSDC is in charge of implementing the scheme.

The government approved Rs 12000 crores in July 2016 for skilling 10 million youth under PMKVY (2016-20) and Rs 10000 crores for skilling 5 million apprentices under the National Apprenticeship Promotion Scheme (NAPS) for the 2016-20 term. The Cabinet authorised two new World Bank-supported initiatives in 2017 totaling Rs. 6,655 crores: Skills Acquisition and Knowledge Awareness for Livelihood Promotion (SANKALP) and Skill Strengthening for Industrial Value Enhancement (STRIVE). SANKALP is a Rs 4,455 crore centrally sponsored programme with a World Bank loan support of Rs 3,300 crores, whilst STRIVE is a Rs 2,200 crore central sector programme with World Bank financial assistance accounting for half of the scheme budget.

1.5.1 A Critique on PMKVY 2.0 (2016-20)

The Pradhan Mantri Kaushal Vikas Yojana (PMKVY) was established in 2015 to encourage and promote skill development in the country by offering free short-term skill training and rewarding it by paying young for skill certification. The overarching goal is to increase youth's employability in order to address the skills gap and meet the industry's demand for trained labour. About 19.85 lakh individuals were trained during the pilot phase (2015-16).

Following the successful implementation of the pilot PMKVY (2015-16), PMKVY 2.0 (2016-20) was started, with stronger alignment with other government of India missions such as Make in India, Digital India, Bharat Mala, Sagar Mala, Swachh Bharat and others. The scheme is based on the Common Norms and has a budget of Rs 12000 crores. Under the direction of the MSDE, the National Skills Development Corporation (NSDC) implements PMKVY.

1.5.2 Objectives of PMKVY 2.0

Under PMKVY 2.0 (2016-20), the following objectives were envisaged:

- Enable and organise a significant number of young people to participate in industry-designed quality skill training, gain employment, and earn a living.
- Increase the productivity of the current workforce and connect skill training with the country's actual needs.
- Encourage the standardisation of the certification process and lay the groundwork for the creation of a skills register.
- Over a four-year period, benefit 10 million young people (2016-2020).

1.5.3 Key Components of the Scheme

1. Short Term Training (STT) - The PMKVY Training Centres (TCs) provide Short-Term Training to candidates who are either school/college dropouts or unemployed. The length of training varies depending on the employment role, but most courses last between 200 and 600 hours (two to 6 months). The training is based on the National Skills Qualification Framework (NSQF), and includes Soft Skills, Entrepreneurship, Financial, and Digital Literacy components. Training Partners assist applicants with job placement after they have completed their examination and certification (TPs).

2. Recognition of Prior Learning (RPL) - The RPL component of the Scheme assesses and certifies individuals with prior learning experience or skills. RPL intends to align the country's unregulated workforce's competencies with the NSQF. The training/orientation lasts anywhere from 12 to 80 hours.

3. Special Projects - The Unique Projects component of PMKVY aims to stimulate trainings in particular regions and premises of government agencies, corporate / industrial bodies, and trainings in special work functions not covered by existing Qualification Packs (QPs)/National Occupational Standards (NOSs). These are the projects that may necessitate some deviance from the PMKVY's Short-Term Training terms and conditions.

Kaushal and Rozgar Mela - The PMKVY's effectiveness depend heavily on social and community mobilisation. The community's active participation provides transparency and accountability, as well as harnessing the community's collective expertise for better functioning. In accordance with this, PMKVY places a premium on the target beneficiaries' participation in a well-defined mobilisation process. Every six months, TPs will hold Kaushal and Rozgar Melas with press/media attention.

1.5.3.1 Highlights of the PMKVY 2.0

PMKVY 2.0 states that the Centre, in collaboration with the States, is putting this plan into action. The scheme is fully funded by the Centre. The components and the targets are given below:

- Centrally Sponsored State Managed (CSSM) -20.50 lacs candidates
- Centrally Sponsored Centrally Managed (CSCM)- 79.50 lacs candidates
- CSSM components were STT and Special Projects while CSCM had STT, RPL and Special Projects.
- It was mandated that 70 percent of the certified candidates must be placed in jobs/self-employment
- Monitoring framework was strengthened and Aadhar Based Attendance System made mandatory.

1.5.4 Training Sectors

The training was given in the following sectors

Table 1.1: Operational Highlights PMKVY 2.0

	As on Mar 31, 2020
Number of operational training centres	10,373
Districts covered	692
Sectors covered	39
Presence in States/UTs	34

NSDC Annual Report 2019-20

https://nsdcindia.org/sites/default/files/files/NSDC-Annual-Report-2019-20.pdf

Figure 1.2: Top 5 Sectors which contribute 52% of trained candidates

The below graph depicts the state wise contribution of top 5 sectors (IT-ITES – 3.82 Lacs, Construction – 1.185 Lacs, Auto – 1.53 Lacs, Healthcare – 1.38 Lacs, Retail – 1.29 Lacs) covered by NSDC Training Partners during FY 2017-18.

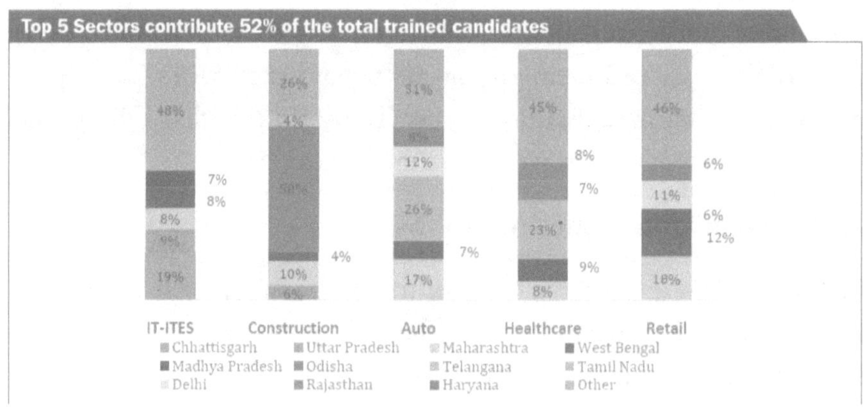

NSDC Annual Report 2019-20

https://nsdcindia.org/sites/default/files/files/NSDC-Annual-Report-2019-20.pdf

1.5.5 Key Stakeholders

The scheme has a number of stakeholders who are responsible for the program's successful implementation. The following are the important stakeholders: -

- ❖ MSDE
- ❖ NSDC: It is the major implementing agency in charge of overseeing and monitoring the central government's many programmes.
- ❖ Sector Skills Councils (SSCs): They are the certifying authority for the STT and certify skilling imparted under PMKVY, other Government schemes and by the industry on the qualification packs. SSCs affiliate training partners and assessment agencies for conducting training and assessment respectively.
- ❖ Training Providers: Once the allocation of the target is done, they establish training centres for those job roles, mobilise and counsel the candidates, train them through SSC certified trainers, get them certified and assist in their placements.
- ❖ Assessment Agencies: Since training must be followed by assessment, it is the obligation of the SSCs to appoint assessment agencies to administer assessments to SSC certified applicants.
- ❖ State Skill Development Missions: They are responsible for PMKVY State component (Centrally Sponsored State Managed (CSSM))
- ❖ Industry: training on Public private Model (PPP), facilitating skill gap studies and jobs.
- ❖ District Administration- facilitates in identification of the job roles for skilling, helping mobilisation, monitoring & evaluation, quality assurance; and facilitation in job placements.
- ❖ UIDAI: for Aadhar enabled Attendance System.
- ❖ Beneficiaries

1.5.6 Implementation of PMKVY

The scheme is being implemented through:

1. **Centrally Sponsored Centrally Managed (CSCM):** National Skill Development Corporation is in charge of this component. Under CSCM, 75 percent of the PMKVY 2016-20 finances and physical targets have been allocated.

2. **Centrally Sponsored State Managed (CSSM):** State governments carry out this component through State Skill Development Missions (SSDMs). CSSM has been allotted 25% of the PMKVY 2016-20 money and related physical targets.

The Haryana Skill Development Mission is in charge of implementing the PMKVY in Haryana.

The complete training programme implementation can be divided into two phases: the preparatory phase and the operational phase.

1.5.6.1 Preparatory phase

The job roles at the preparatory phase are mentioned as follows: -

Figure 1.3: Steps in the Implementation Process - Preparatory Phase

Steps in the Preparatory Phase

Step 1	Step 2	Step 3	Step 4	Step 5
On boarding of SSCs	Finalization of Job Roles	Granting Affiliation to Training Partners (TPs)	Registration of Assessment Agencies	Monitoring Plan .

1.5.6.2 Operational phase

After this phase is completed, the operational phase begins. Actual implementation should take place at this phase, and the duties of the many stakeholders are substantially greater.

Figure 1.4: Steps in the Implementation Process - Operational Phase

Steps in the Operational Phase

Step 1	Step 2	Step 3	Step 4	Step 5	Step 6	Step 7
Allocation of Job role wise target to SSCs and TPs	Mobilization of candidates to be facilitated by the state governments	Enrolment of the candidates and uploading information in SDMS by TPs database SDMS	Imparting of training for the assigned job roles by TPs	Assessment and uploading the results in SDMS. by the assessors on successful completion of the training.	Certifications to the trainees by SSCs.	Disbursement of reward money to the trainees by NSDC.

1.5.7 Challenges of the PMKVY

There are several challenges with the PMKVY since its inception, which is explained asunder:

- The scale, speed and standard under PMKVY is not up to the desired level due to the paucity of certified trainers, assessors, quality infrastructure, participation by the industry and funding (public and private).
- The placement rates for jobs of skilled and certified under PMKVY is fewer than 55 percent, as against a target of 70%.
- The youth is not inspired to undergo skills training under PMKVY due to poor job placement and skill premium in salaries. In the Info Age, the candidates wish to learn and earn on the job; knowledge could be through blended learning.
- Industry does not see an advantage in employing a skilled and certified workforce.
- Cognitive and soft skills of the PMKVY skilled manpower are inadequate to improve their employability.

- Emphasis under PMKVY is inadequate for future skills. STEM education is inadequate to meet future skills.
- International mobility of the skilled workforce does not have the required emphasis under PMKVY.

Despite these challenges, so far, the performance of PMKVY has been satisfactory. Since 5 years of inception of the PMKVY, (PMKVY 1.0 & 2.0) over 88.76 lakh candidates have been enrolled; of these over 79.74 lakhs certified and have been certified till February 2018. Placements performance has been under 57 % (as on 19 July 2020).

1.5.8 Rolling out of the PMKVY 3.0

On January 15, 2021, the MSDE announced the third phase of its flagship initiative, Pradhan Mantri Kaushal Vikas Yojana (PMKVY 3.0).

Like in the case of its predecessor scheme, PMKVY 3.0 also has three subcomponents:

- **Short term Training (STT)** for the re-skilling of high school/ college dropouts and unemployed kids
- **Recognition of Prior Learning (RPL)** to acknowledge existing skills and Special Projects (SPL) to meet vulnerable groups' skilling needs and allow for some flexibility in the delivery of Short-Term Training (STT).
- Special Projects

1.5.9 Objectives of PMKVY 3.0 (2020-21)

The following are the scheme's main principles:

- From the former training provider-driven paradigm to a learner/ trainee-centric paradigm.
- Planning from the ground up, with district-level plans serving as the primary implementers.
- Enhance the involvement of states and local governments in the scheme's implementation. Providing handholding, strategic, and

financial support to District Skill Committees (DSCs), State Skill Development Missions (SSDMs), and the State Directorate of Technical Education or Skill Development.

- Create a pool of certified trainers for whom direct financing for Training of Trainers (ToT) programmes will be provided.
- Major emphasis on up-skilling / reskilling with a focus on future skills (industry 4.0) courses to boost existing labour productivity.
- Focus on online/digital training to reach a bigger audience.
- Introduce major improvements to the assessment environment, such as the usage of Common Assessment Centres (CACs) and online assessment tools.
- Large-scale grass-roots publicity (including the distribution of booklets and pamphlets) Media Campaigns /Awareness Programs will be implemented.

1.5.10 Support structure

The following support system has been planned to help the programme accomplish its goals:

- At the district level, begin the process of establishing nodal skill information and service centres.
- Create awareness about skill development training and mobilise youth to take advantage of it in order to gain employment and support their families.
- Continuously conduct a skill gap study and analysis to address industry demands and current market demand.
- Encourage more standardisation across the entire training process and establish a skills registry.
- Strive to establish cutting-edge, long-term skill training centres.
- Encourage the creation of Centres of Excellence through Sector Skill Councils (SSCs) (CoE).
- Private sector engagement in PMKVY 3.0 should be pushed even more, with a larger emphasis on industry training.

1.5.11 Training Target

Due to the fact that PMKVY 3.0 is a demand-driven scheme, training targets can be dynamically set based on recommendations. Based on the lessons learned from PMKVY 2.0 (2016-20), the following are the tentative training goals till March 31, 2021:

Table 1.2: Training Target under PMKVY 3.0

Sl.No.	Types of Training under PMKVY 3.0	No of Candidates (in lakh)
1	PMKVY Short Term Training (STT)	2.2
2	PMKVY Recognition of Prior Learning (RPL)	5.8
	Total	8

1.6 Case Selection

Haryana is a state with a rich cultural heritage and a thriving agricultural sector. It is bordered on the north by Himachal Pradesh, on the east by Uttar Pradesh, on the west by Punjab, and on the south by Rajasthan. The State is surrounded on three sides by the National Capital, Delhi. It covers 44,212 square kilometres, accounting for 1.3 percent of the country's total size. This is depicted on the following map: -

Figure 1.5: Status of PMKVY Short Term Training Programmes in Haryana

Source: http://www.pmkvyofficial.org/Dashboard.aspx accessed on 28th Feb 2021

Haryana contributes a substantial amount of wheat and rice to the Central Pool, a national food grain repository system. Haryana is India's fourth-largest cotton producer. Haryana has also made significant progress in the industrial sector. Automotive, information technology, agriculture, and petrochemicals are the major sectors in Haryana. The State is the largest car hub in the country, and it is a favourite destination for car majors and auto-component makers. The Panipat Refinery (IOCL), located in Panipat, is South Asia's second largest refinery. The state government has made a commitment to fostering a forward-thinking corporate climate. Haryana's structural shift from an agrarian to an industrial state, with a burgeoning services sector. Despite being a tiny state in terms of geography, Haryana's contribution to the national gross domestic product at constant (2011-12) prices has been assessed at 3.8 percent in the 2019-20 Quick Estimates.

1.6.1 Reasons for selecting Haryana

The effectiveness of the PMKVY has been considered in the case of select districts of Haryana primarily from the youth's aspiration and trainees' perspective. The reasons for selecting Haryana in this study is due to the fact that Haryana seems to hold a lot of potential, not lagging far behind the envisioned target of skilling youths and the youths in Haryana constitute a sizable proportion of employable population who can be trained and empowered.

As per the statistics provided in Haryana PMKVY Dashboard, it is found that 58.18% is a current placement percentage (as on Feb 2021). So, it is viable to conduct an empirical study to assess the effectiveness of PMKVY in select districts of Haryana. The pertinent points about

PMKVY as implemented in Haryana are enumerated below: -

1.6.2 PMKVY 2.0 in Haryana

PMKVY 2016-20 is the MSDE's flagship skill development programme. This is a grant-based programme that provides free skill development training and certification in over 350 career roles in order to boost youth employability. It is necessary to record these facts in the context of the investigation. First, the Haryana Skill Development Mission is implementing this programme in the state of Haryana.

1.6.2.1 Eligibility of Candidates

Any unemployed or school/college dropout, regardless of his urban/rural background, can benefit from this programme.

1.6.2.2 Progress of PMKVY in Haryana

The Year wise detail of PMKVY in Haryana is mentioned in the table given below:

Table 1.3: Year wise detail of PMKVY in Haryana

Name of Scheme	Year	Target	No. of Persons Enrolled	No. of Persons Trained	No. of Persons Assessed	No. of Trainees Certified	No. of Trainees got placed
Pradhan Mantri Kaushal Vikas Yojana (PMKVY)	2016-20	38560	36029	30929	25294	21949	6478
	2020-21	2058	In principle approval has been received from MoSDE, GoI, but guidelines & budget is yet to be received from GoI.				

Name of Scheme	Year	Target	No. of Persons Enrolled	No. of Persons Trained	No. of Persons Assessed	No. of Trainees Certified
Recognition of Prior Learning (RPL) under State Scheme (SURYA)	2018-19	2000	55	55	55	48
	2019-20		200	200	0	0
Recognition of Prior Learning (RPL) under PMKVY	2020-21	4400	In-principle approval has been received from MoSDE, GoI, but guidelines & budget is yet to be received from GoI			

Source: Skill Development and Industrial Training Department Haryana

1.7 Objectives of the Study

The major goal of this research is to undertake a comprehensive evaluation of PMKVY Training Effectiveness from the perspective of the young in a few Haryana districts.

The following are the objectives of this research:-

1. To understand the demographic profile of beneficiaries under the PMKVY scheme in select districts of Haryana.
2. To understand the awareness and its association with participation of the trainee youth / beneficiaries in Kaushal Melas with respect to PMKVY training.
3. To understand the beneficiary's Aspirations for the training sector and Training imparted under PMKVY.
4. To understand the sub-components in the delivery mechanisms of PMKVY Training.
5. To identify and validate the beneficiary's perceptions on the components of PMKVY Trainings
6. To understand the relationship of the components of PMKVY Training with effectiveness of PMKVY Trainings (in terms of skills enhancement, satisfaction and standard of living)

1.7.1 Hypotheses of the Study

Objective 2: To understand the awareness and its association with participation of the trainee youth / beneficiaries in Kaushal Melas with respect to PMKVY training.

Hypotheses

H1: There is no significant association between beneficiary's awareness on the Training Sector of Interest with their participation in Kaushal Mela under PMKVY.

H2: There is no significant association between beneficiary's awareness on eligibility criteria for the enrollment in PMKVY training with their participation in Kaushal Mela under PMKVY.

H3: There is no link between beneficiaries' awareness of the training centres available in their district and their participation in Kaushal Mela under PMKVY.

H4: There is no significant association between beneficiary's awareness that PMKVY training is free with their participation in Kaushal Mela under PMKVY.

Objective 6: To understand the relationship of the components of PMKVY Training with effectiveness of PMKVY Trainings (in terms of skills enhancement, satisfaction and standard of living)

Hypotheses

H5: There is no significant relationship between Training Quality and skill enhancement of PMKVY

H6: There is no significant relationship between Resources and Support and skill enhancement of PMKVY

H7: There is no significant relationship between Infrastructure and skill enhancement of PMKVYH8: There is no significant relationship between Training Quality and Satisfaction of Beneficiaries

H9: There is no significant relationship between Resources & Support and Satisfaction of Beneficiaries

H10: There is no significant relationship between Infrastructure and Satisfaction of Beneficiaries

H11: There is no significant relationship between Training Quality and Standard of Living of Beneficiaries

H12: There is no significant relationship between Resources and Support and Standard of Living of Beneficiaries

H13: There is no significant relationship between Infrastructure and Standard of Living of Beneficiaries

1.8 Research Methodology

In this study, a 'descriptive' research design will be employed to assess the PMKVY training and its efficiency from the perspective of the youth trainees/beneficiaries in a few Haryana districts. In other words, it will look into the PMKVY training's effectiveness on terms of impact results in Haryana's young skilling and employability.

In Haryana, 13 districts representing rural, semi-urban, and urban belts were chosen as the sampling frame for the study. The 'stratified random sample method' was utilised in the investigation. The selection criteria for each district skill centre were set at 10% of the computed sample size. As a result, this study's sample size was reduced to 816 trainees/beneficiaries. The required information was elicited from both primary and secondary sources of data in order to arrive at the study's conclusions.

The data is quantitatively examined using the SPSS 25 statistical software. To make significant inferences for the study, descriptive and inferential statistics were employed for data analysis. For demographic profiling of the trainees, descriptive statistical approaches such as "frequency and mean values" were used. In addition, inferential statistics were utilised in the study (Correlation, Chi-square analysis, ANOVA, Multiple Regression).

1.9 Significance of the Study

As discussed in the research problem statement, the basic tenet of this study is drawn from the growing importance of the realization of harnessing demographic dividend through skill development of the youth. The PMKVY stands to fulfill this major aim of the skilling ecosystem. In the first place, the significance of the study stems from the basic theme of the study and the fact that there is hardly any empirical study conducted so far in Haryana. This study is driven from the trainee/youth beneficiary's perspective. So, the first-hand information will be elicited which will help the policy makers in further improving the PMKVY training in Haryana and other locations as well.

Another important significance of the study is the comprehensive nature with which it has covered not only the PMKVY training program but also the outcome benefits as perceived by the trainees who were enrolled and undergone training. So, it reflects the ground reality of the PMKVY training from the beneficiary's perspective which is very important for the successful implementation of any training program.

The study saliently addresses the youth awareness and mobilization link, their perception on the different components of the PMKVY training (related to training quality content, resources, and support facilities along with the infrastructural facilities at the training centres in their district), and relationship between the PMKVY training components and perceived outcome benefits accruing to the trainees.

This extends the scope of the study in evaluating the efficacy of the PMKVY training from the trainee's perspective. It will majorly contribute through reflecting whether the youth are aptly mobilized and encouraged to undertake training in important job roles/sectors of their interest and are they satisfied with the training undergone. It will also address the pertinent issue of whether the youths have gained on skill enhancement to be able to venture out beyond the traditional paradigm of conventional skill and also breaking the gender stereotype in choosing skill trades.

1.10 Outline of Thesis

The thesis entitled, **"A Study of the Effectiveness of Pradhan Mantri Kaushal Vikas Yojana in Select Districts of Haryana"** has been subdivided in following chapters, as:

Chapter 1: Introduction

Chapter 1 presents an overview of the study detailing its rationale, background, the problem statement, research objectives along with an overview on the research methodology and significance of the study.

Chapter 2: Review of Literature

This chapter presents a detailed review of extant studies in a systematic manner that finally culminates in the research gaps setting the foundation for this study.

Chapter 3: Research Design and Methodology

In this chapter, research design and research methodology used for this study are explained. It also enumerates the research process as adopted in the study along with the objectives and hypotheses of the study. The chapter also elaborates upon the sampling methodology, data collection methodology and techniques for data analysis used in the study.

Chapter 4: Analysis and Findings

In this chapter, detailed discussion dwells upon the analysis as per the study objectives. It elaborates the demographic profile of the trainee/youth beneficiaries, their awareness level on the PMKVY training, accessibility, sectors where training is imparted and the various components of the PMKV training program. Further, as per the hypotheses of the study, the analysis details the trainees perceived benefit/outcomes of the PMKVY training in improving their skills, standard of living and their satisfaction.

Chapter 5: Conclusions and Recommendations

This chapter presents final conclusions and recommendations in the light of the study findings while pointing out the limitations and highlighting the scope for future research studies. In addition, this chapter entails both the policy and operational recommendations that will pave the way forward for the PMKVY.

Chapter 2

The Context

2.1 Introduction

A review of the literature is a critical component of any research since it highlights previous work undertaken by diverse scholars in the same topic. It enables the researcher to dissect the study problem and scenario in order to generate new concepts, explanations, and hypotheses. This chapter provides a full analysis of the existing 'Literature Review,' focusing on the central issue of the 'learning environment', which serves as the study's foundation. A thorough examination of the literature was undertaken primarily to determine the study's variables and research technique, which resulted in the identification of research gaps at the chapter's conclusion.

Given the critical nature of skill development in enhancing youth employability and filling the demand-supply gap in the existing labor market, and more specifically in tapping the demographic dividend of India's young population from the informal sector, this chapter highlights key studies that contribute to the existing literature and knowledge base. It is necessary to highlight the Government of India's skill development programs, particularly through the flagship program Pradhan Mantri Kaushal Vikas Yojana (PMKVY) and PMKVY 2.0, which were extensively discussed in Chapter 1 to provide context for the study. The review of literature in this chapter includes discussions of the skilling requirements and the PMKVY 2.0 to accomplish this goal through the use of specific research studies conducted by researchers as well as reports from government and eminent research bodies at the national and international levels.

2.2 The Context

The extant literature studies emphasizing the need of skill-based training to youth for enhancing their employability and skills are mentioned chronologically, in descending order, to purport its importance and latest developments, in the following paragraphs, as: -

UNDP, CII, AICTE, Association of Indian Universities, Wheebox, India Skills Report (2021). The report highlights the demand and supply of the talent post COVID (first wave), emphasis on digital excellence, remote working, mitigation of health hazards for the workforce, new jobs, substantial growth in Pharma and healthcare, internet business, logistics, software/hardware and IT and BFSI sectors. Due to a pandemic caused by economic COVID-19, daily wage workers, contractual labour, and the self -employed have been hit the hardest. The practice of virtual hiring, remote working, online learning and assessments picked up pace. The youth employability dipped from 45.9% from last year's 46.2%. Candidates from Maharashtra, Tamil Nadu and Karnataka had the highest employable talent.

World Economic Forum, the Future of Jobs Report. (2020) The report elaborates on the unabated growth in the technology, automation, economic recession due to pandemic caused by COVID -19, reduced workforce due to technology disruption, emerging jobs for tomorrow, increase in online white collared workforce, increase on online learning and training, adverse impact on low job workers, increase in emphasis on investment on human capital, public sector support on skilling and re-skilling. Impetus is being given to increase the digitalization of work processes, provide more opportunities to work remotely, accelerate automation of tasks etc. Technologies likely to be adopted by 2025 are Encryption and cyber security, cloud computing distributed ledger technology (block chain), robots, 3D and 4d printing, internet of things and connected devices etc.

Grant Thornton, Skilling Ecosystem in India (2020) the publication emphasizes on unlocking the potential of youth, harnessing the demographic dividend and capitalising on the workforce by vocational education and training. The report discusses the transformation brought in the institutional mechanism from 2009 onwards to keep pace with the skilling requirement. Interventions brought upon by the Government to strengthen the skill ecosystem such as institutional strengthening at the National, State and District levels, rolling out schemes such as National Skill Certification and Reward (STAR), Pradhan Mantri Kaushal Vikas Yojana (PMKVY), National Apprenticeship promotion Scheme (NAPS), Deen Dayal Upadhyaya Gramin Kaushalya Yojana (DDU-GKY) etc. were discussed.

UNDP, CII, AICTE, Association of Indian Universities, Wheebox. (2020) The report delves upon the changing landscape **of** the skill ecosystem due to, political environment and growth-oriented initiatives, industry 4.0 students aspirations, technological advances, future jobs and offerings by the educational institutions. The growth sectors are BFSI, IT/ITES, BPOs/KPOs and internet business. The talent has to re-skill to meet the changing industry environment. Maharashtra, Tamil Nadu will be leading the hiring followed by Delhi.

In a recent study, **Thakur, K.S. and Agrawal, Mini (2019)** conducted a study to determine the impact of the PMKVY on enhancing youth productivity in the Gwalior region. The data was acquired through questionnaires performed at the PMKVY training center in Gwalior, India, using non-probability sampling. A total of 1197 trainees were included in the study. The study's findings demonstrate that training improves abilities, improves performance, fosters entrepreneurship, and allows people to make a living.

Through personal interviews and observations of the respondents, **Bhuvana S., Kavya, and Geetanjali P. (2019)** conducted the study to analyze the effectiveness of skill development programs for upgrading their talents. The findings highlighted a number of challenges, including a lack of employment opportunities and time to master the topics. It alluded to the necessity for new courses, such as the fashion industry and cinematography, among others.

Ramaswamy B, Pushpa Sasikala and Gururaj M.B. (2019) in their book on skill development in India, the authors emphasize on harnessing the demographic dividend of India. Impetus to be given n vocational education in schools, colleges and universities. The writers dwell upon the difference between knowledge and skills, the latter being important to enhance employment. Critical thinking, creativity, collaboration, communication skills, technology, information literacy, social skills can help the students to remain competitive.

According to the **World Bank's 2019** report, many occupations now, and many more in the near future, will demand a unique set of talents—a mixture of technological expertise, problem-solving abilities, and critical thinking, as well as soft skills such as perseverance, collaboration, and empathy. Workers in the gig economy are likely to have multiple gigs throughout their careers, which implies they must be lifelong learners. While innovation will continue to increase, developing countries will need to respond quickly to assure their continued competitiveness in the future economy.

According to the **MSDE report (2019)**, the ministry has worked extensively with a number of nations to facilitate technology transfer for skill training, trainer training, and the establishment of models and centers of excellence. We are seeking active participation in the area of fostering international mobility through the establishment of transnational standards.

NSDC report (2019) covers PMKVY extensively and highlights the progress attained through Kaushal Kendras, India International Skill Centers, Apprenticeship programs (NAPS), Building Private Sector Capacity, Creating Enabling systems, Collaborative Programs For Inclusive & Sustainable Development, Technological Interventions, Industry partnerships and CSR, Disadvantaged Communities: Affirmative Action, Supporting National Flagship Schemes, International collaborations, Technical Intern Training Program (TITP) with Japan, India Skills & World Skills and Analytics & Impact Assessment.

In the report in Business Standard (2019), it is presented that the Indian government's aim **is** to skill 10 million youth by 2020 falling 64% short of target. In November 2018, just over 3.6 million people had been enrolled in the PMKVY by November 30 which is much shorter than the target.

Wipro-NASSCOM (2019), in the paper, "Talent and New ways of working in the age of digital transformation" highlighted the importance of digital transformation as a business strategy for growth and profitability. So, it is imperative to keep pace with the ever-evolving customers' expectations, ahead of competitors by continuously improving their products and services. This is true for all firms, including the SMEs in the Indian scenario.

PWC, FICCI (2019) according to the research, "Fast Forward. - Relevant Skills for a Flourishing Indian Economy," global megatrends such as rapid urbanisation, demographic transformations, and shifts in global economic power, political shifts, and technology are shaping how businesses operate today. According to the report, the number of rule- and routine-based jobs will decline significantly as a result of growing human-machine interaction and the availability of adaptive and intelligent technology.

Rashmi Dewangan (2018) presented a literature analysis of the Pradhan Mantri Kaushal Vikas Yojana (PMKVY) initiative, highlighting its role, primary features, and critical contributions to rural youths' skill development and empowerment. The study's findings indicate that the primary objective of this certification scheme is to enable a large number of young people to participate in industry-relevant skill training courses. It advocated conducting similar research to examine the success of this skill development system across states and also advocated conducting comparison research on short-term training and prior learning recognition under the PMKVY

Ansari and Khan (2018) did a study titled "Role of Education and Skill Development in Promoting Employment in India" with the goal of examining the current state of contemporary education in relation to skill development. Secondary data was gathered to accomplish this purpose through published studies, polls, books, significant websites, and media stories, among other sources. In accordance with the study's aims, the descriptive research design was used. It is concluded that India's skill development is vital from both a socioeconomic and demographic standpoint. It is critical for poverty alleviation, increasing competitiveness and employability, and promoting youth self-entrepreneurship. With this new approach, our economy is certain to fulfil its objectives. Every year, approximately 12 million young people in India enter the labor force with inadequate education and rudimentary work skills. If they are unable to find work owing to a lack of skills, widespread social unrest may ensue. To advance further toward a knowledge-based economy, to encourage industrial development, and to achieve high economic growth, it must significantly boost its investment in education and training for the young, while maintaining a proper balance.

Singh and Kaur (2018) conducted a study titled "A Study on Skill Development in the Paint and Coating Industry" with the objective of determining the reasons for the paint industry's skills shortage and potential solutions. To accomplish this goal, a self-administered questionnaire was used to collect data from 130 painters in the Kurukshetra area. The findings indicate that a lack of formal training and insufficient provisions for painters' training are the primary factors in the paint industry's skills shortfall. Additionally, the results indicate that the paint business is experiencing a skill deficit. The findings demonstrated that training had a favourable and significant effect on workforce performance, despite a lack of formal training without official certification and painters lacking sufficient knowledge and abilities, resulting in substandard performance. Furthermore, knowledge and ability of new equipment and procedures in painting work were lacking, and the work environment was hazardous due to lax safety standards and the lack of painters' insurance plans.

Sanghi, Sunita, Parvathy, Lakshmi, Khurana, Sakshi (2018) emphasized the importance of Niti Aayog-India identifying and developing Skill Development Indicators in their study. The OECD pioneered such initiatives by establishing the World Indicators of Skills for Employment (WISE) in close collaboration with the World Bank, ETF, ILO, and

UNESCO. Using this framework, an attempt has been made to establish indicators that address various difficulties associated with increasing the efficiency of the Indian skill ecosystem in terms of matching talents across sectors/regions in order to maximize the potential of our youth.

Vyas (2018) in the study highlighted the role and importance of skill development leading to women empowerment. It has been said that for any socio-economic development women empowerment is essential. Skill development is vital to get success which improves productivity, employability and earning opportunities of women. It enables them to identify their skills, knowledge and abilities to make their own decisions. It has been considered as a growth process for women which consists of awareness, attainment and actualization which act as the bridge between job and workforce. It has been said that the concept of skill development needs to move beyond the technical and managerial skills which consists of political and life skills. Digital platforms can be used for women empowerment. As India is trying to move towards a knowledge-based economy, it is important for the country to give emphasis on the progression of the skills which have the relevance to bring the emerging economy.

The Ministry of Skill Development and Entrepreneurship (MSDE) (2018) in a report titled "Skill India-Highlights 2018," reaffirmed the importance of skills and emphasized the National Skills Qualification Framework's primary skill development programs (NSQF). Regarding the PMKVY, the report indicated that roughly 40.5 lakh candidates had been trained under Short Term Training and Recognition of Prior Learning up to 2017. People Strong, Wheebox, CII, UNDP, AICTE, and AIU (2020) in India Skills Report 2020 emphasize the importance of talent reinventing itself with great agility in order to remain relevant in a changing landscape of work prospects.

National Council of Applied Economic Research (NCAER) (2018) study further stressed the critical nature of resolving India's vicious cycle of low skill levels and a scarcity of excellent jobs if the country is to avert a job crisis. There is considerable work to be done to balance the supply and demand for skills. As a result, considerable attention must be paid to skill learning, skill matching, and skill anticipation.

UNDP, Wheebox, People Strong, CII (2018) covered a wide range of topics in their report, titled "India Skills Report 2018," including - Employment and Hiring Trends, Automation and its Impact on Industry, Future Skills and Future Jobs, preparing for the Future of Work, Apprenticeship - Preparing young talent, and Preferences - Candidates and Employers' Job Preferences. Additionally, the paper underlined the role of government and non-government entities in enhancing youth' skills and employability.

Ernst & Young (2018) stated in the study report that India falls significantly behind other countries in imparting skill training. Only 10% of the country's overall workforce obtains skill training. Additionally, 80% of new workers lack access to skill training.

Singh, Ashutosh Prasad (2018) presented a report on the 'Sharda Prasad Committee on Skill India Reforms' the presentation highlighted the various issues faced by vocational education and training and the suggested reforms.

Sanjiv Kataria (2018) studied ways in which India might increase the employability of its jobless young in his study. According to the study, the primary reason for youth unemployment in India is the countries excessively controlled higher education system, which maintains obsolete curricula and also stifles innovation. According to the researchers, employability does not simply refer to the ability to obtain work; it also refers to providing young men and women with the skills, information, and tools necessary to thrive in their jobs.

Patnaik, Ipseeta Satpathy, and Snigdha Suhagi (2018) sought to understand the role of ITES in PMKVY in their work. Secondary data was used to accomplish this purpose. The study discovered that PMKVY is critical since it enhances the workforce's abilities and that ITES is vital in its implementation.

Ganesh (2017) in the study attempted to identify the deficiencies in the context of developing 'Smart India" and also suggested ways to bridge the gap between skills and employability. It has stated in the study that to attain the competitive periphery as a skilled nation, India needs an industry- ready and as well as a job -ready workforce. Thus, there is a great demand for employment in future. But as of now less than 4% of the workforce is skilled. So, there is a huge need for skill training. Indian government till now has undertaken many initiatives to give training to the unskilled workforce. PMKVY is one of those initiatives which have started in the year 2015.

Shrivastav and Jatav (2017) did a study titled "An Analysis of the Benefits and Obstacles of Skilling India" with the objective of assessing the opportunities and challenges associated with in India. The study's specific aims were to assess India's experience with skill development and the obstacles associated with it in terms of financial resources. Additionally, the study analyzed the general state of available skill capacity, skill requirements, skill gaps, and GoI-led skill development programs. To accomplish this goal, data was acquired from secondary sources, namely the Ministry of Micro, Small, and Medium-Sized Enterprises (MSME), the websites of the relevant startups, the websites of other government organizations, and their annual reports. The study's findings indicated the various programs established by the Government of India to create job opportunities aligned with the changing industrial skill requirements. Additionally, the study stated that India's current skill development policy requires significant change and reform, including simplification of the 'institutional structure' through increased investment in training infrastructure and an emphasis on supporting a casual labor force, which should be accompanied by incentives for private sector participation.

Prasad and Purohit (2017) published a paper titled "Skill Development, Employability, and Entrepreneurship in India: A Study." The study's aims were to determine the effects of the 'Make in India' initiative on employability and to analyze India's current skill development status. This exploratory research study makes use of secondary data and materials gathered from libraries, pertinent books, journals, magazines, and articles, among other sources. According to the findings, in order for the "Make in India" initiative to succeed, youths must be provided with formal education, technical, and vocational training in order to meet global industrial and market demands. Despite numerous efforts and investments in developing the skills of a large worker force, the system has significant flaws. India also needs knowledge workers with ICT skills, problem-solving abilities, analytical abilities, and effective communication abilities. Vocational education should begin in high school, and students should be prepared for the workforce by designing professional courses such as engineering and MBA in such a way that they include comprehensive on-the-job training. Training must be improved in terms of both standards and quality. Soft skills training in conjunction with technical skills training will yield the desired results.

Chandrasekaran and Anbuthambi (2017) provided an in-depth analysis of the current state of skill development programs in rural areas of the country in their paper. It stressed the critical relevance of cost effectiveness in such skill development programs and the need to provide equal opportunity without regard for gender and also by addressing the concerns of physical and financial inclusion (disability) for all genders and social groups. In the future, skill development may aid in the development of an increasing number of businesses.

Divyaranjani and Rajasekar (2017) evaluated the effectiveness of training in terms of overall workforce development. Using data from 456 workers in the automobile industry in Chennai, they discovered the critical nature of training and development efforts in terms of enhancing worker skills, capability, and productivity.

FICCI and KPMG Report (2017) has analyzed the skill ecosystem of India. According to the report, India occupies a unique and special place in the global skilling ecosystem. To maintain balance with the global activities, domestic and industrial output is crucially needed. The Ministry of labour and employment has set up many Industrial Training Institutes (ITIs) and has also set up councils for the certification of those trainees. To define the road map for skill development, the Government established the National Skills Qualification Framework. There is a tremendous need to extend consciousness about the need for skilling and the responsibilities lie on all the stakeholders such as Central and State Governments, industries etc. Industries also need educated personnel as it will increase the productivity of companies. The industries should work closely with SSCs. They also need to be concerned about the participation of the employees regarding skill development initiatives.

Skill India Report (2017) presented that there is a need for major intensification of the skill landscape through quantitative and qualitative analysis of the demand and supply sides of the labour market. This analysis examined the employability factors of youth from diverse educational backgrounds across the country, as well as the demands and expectations of employers. It is also highlighted that digital transformation is challenging the conventional way of working and the employers from the industries are demanding readily available knowledge or skill which is suitable for the present job scenario. This report has given special focus on skilling and reskilling of the employees. This report has also emphasized on women employability.

Sharma & Sharma (2017) has reported different statistics on recent economic trends of India. From the recent report it can be seen that the economic growth is declining in recent times. During the last few years, the growth of Indian economy has not been as per expectation. The growth of the country depends largely on the service sector alone. But in the last few years, the growth has not been documented properly. That is why in the case of employment, the challenge continues. The most important challenge is the nature of the Indian labour market which is mostly informal in nature. It is quite obvious that these informal laborers are neither entitled to receive job security nor social benefits that are meant for formal sector workers. It is to be noted that only providing skill training will not improve the situation. Skill training should come with suitable policies that can change the business scenario.

Agrawal & Agrawal (2017) discussed the importance of vocational training to prioritize the existing skill gap the country is facing. The aim is to create a pool of skilled workforce so that they can act as a resource in the existing market. The purpose is to find out the relationship of the skills to performance which needs to be mapped to the demand of the employers. It has tried to understand the importance of an array of different entry-level workplace skills and performance of those skills. It has been mentioned that in designing the measures the requirements of students with special educational requirements should be unambiguously taken into account. It has been noted that the acknowledgment of informally acquired job-related skills is a long and behind schedule step. It has been suggested that there is a need to commence synchronized skills corroboration processes to make the skills useful for employees.

OECD Report (2016) underlined the structural changes occurring in the economy as a result of globalization and their effect on the workforce. Historically, the majority of jobs were labor-intensive, and people learnt their trades solely through experience. Numerous structural adjustments have occurred in the global economy, many of which have had a direct influence on people who work in industries with their conventional knowledge and experience. As a result, jobs are getting more competitive, and a new period called has emerged. Skill-based jobs began to gain traction, and suddenly, a gap developed because the workforce lacked the necessary abilities to adapt to employment market changes. Information technology has begun to play a big role as well, and its adoption has become a fundamental objective for every employer. Additionally, the survey argues that adaptability has become a critical standard for both current and future employees. This should be accomplished through an organized and formal system of skill-based education. Unless and until this mechanism is established, the sector will be unable to develop a robust workforce with the specialized skills required by business.

Raju, Abbaiah & Gudavalli (2016) has discussed the role of IT in the education sector. It is true that today in all fields there is an involvement of Technology. It's true that imparting instruction using computer technology is beneficial to students. There are larger benefits of technology assault into the management function of the institutions. It has been suggested that ICT training should be incorporated into the curriculum right from the school level to make future job seekers suitable to the current job situation. Otherwise, there will be skill shortages between the supply and the demand of the employers.

Nandi (2016) has depicted the need for entrepreneurship and skill development in the current employment scenario and the gaps present in skill development issues. The paper throws challenges towards the existing education system. If the aim of the individual is to become an entrepreneur, the challenge remains whether the system has the option or not. If we go into the details of the education policy, till date no such things are witnessed. Most of the time the education policy is traditional in nature and it does not have the capacity to train the people who want to do business on its own. Specific training courses are there but these are beyond the reach of the people who actually need it. This gap in entrepreneurial training is another challenge.

Singh and Sanjeev (2016) did a study titled "Need for Re-Skill Training in Support of the Make in India Initiative" with the objective of determining the elements influencing an employee's attitude toward skill training in a business. To accomplish this, an empirical study was undertaken of information technology (IT) companies located in Delhi and the National Capital Region (NCR), with data collected via a standardized questionnaire distributed to the organization's executives. According to the study's findings, CEOs agreed that rekilling is critical for job advancement and also assists them in learning new technology and abilities. Additionally, it offers them enhanced growth prospects and improves the organization's overall performance. According to the research, elements such as need-based training, appropriate re-skilling, soft skill training, value addition, updated knowledge, and advanced growth all influence employee attitudes toward re-skilling. The study indicated that it is critical to provide employees with the appropriate skills in order to increase their employment chances.

Hazarika (2016) did a study titled "Skill Development for Rural Entrepreneurship: A Case Study of the State Institute of Rural Development (SIRD), Assam" with the objective of assessing the State Institute of Rural

Development's various skill development initiatives for rural entrepreneurship. The purpose of this study was to examine the function of training and its effect on starting businesses in rural areas, as well as to suggest strategies to boost entrepreneurship development through institutional support in rural Assam. The data was gathered from 40 rural entrepreneurs (men and women) who established their businesses following training at the State Institute of Rural Development's (SIRD) Amoni Growth Centre in Assam's Nagaon district. The study's findings suggest that overall employment in the sample units has climbed to 23% since their inception. Apart from the increase in income, it has been discovered that 67 percent of entrepreneurs think that their standard of living has increased. Additionally, these entrepreneurs enhanced their leadership abilities through various training programs, and they gained confidence in approaching financing institutions. Additionally, the data indicated that 59% of them had enhanced their technical skills with the assistance of trainers and that 52% were capable of efficiently allocating existing resources. Numerous female entrepreneurs have also built successful small businesses to supplement their income.

Pandey (2016) conducted a study titled "Improving Skill Development and Employability Potential through Higher Education, Research, and Innovations in India" with the goal of identifying gaps between government and private programs in the areas of skill development, vocational education, and entrepreneurship. Additionally, it explored the importance of incorporating higher education into the purview of the National Skill Development Corporation, UGC. The study discovered that the private sector is critical for bridging the gaps in government programs. However, innovation is lacking in skill development programs. Almost every course and curriculum is designed to meet industrial needs. Additionally, the study identified a critical demand for experienced trainers at all levels who can work full time in institutes and devote their complete attention to enrolled candidates. Finally, the study identified shortcomings in the capacity and quality of training infrastructure and outputs, an insufficient focus on workforce ambitions, a lack of certification and consistent standards, and a glaring lack of attention to the unorganized sector.

Patnaik et al. (2016) emphasized the necessity of skill development for MSME sectors, the majority of which are labor intensive but lack the education and training necessary to adapt to production shifts. According to the study, the only way to transform the sector is through 'value-added education.' As a result, the GoI has resorted to enhancing skills through the assistance of partner institutions in MSMEs. By 2022, it is argued, this sector should be capable of implementing required changes in the workforce development process with the assistance of training institutes. However, the focus at the moment is on identifying the skill gap and establishing an appropriate skill training program.

Deka and Batra (2016) did a study titled "The Scope of Skill Development and Employability of Indian Workers in the Context of Make in India: A Study" with the objective of performing an exhaustive evaluation of the literature on the influence of the "Make in India" initiative on employability. Additionally, it was meant to determine whether skill development strategies would aid in bridging the gap between existing and required capabilities for the Indian workforce. The study is based on a survey of secondary data from libraries, famous journals and publications, and government portals such as "Make in India," "Skill India," and others. The study's findings indicate that "Make in India" has the potential to create new industrial skill requirements in India. Additionally, it provided an overview of the available skill capacity, skill requirements, skill gap, and skill development programs undertaken by the Government of India.

The study, titled "Skill Development: A Way to Leverage India's Demographic Dividend," was done by **Misra (2015).** According to the report, the primary objective of the 'skill development mission' was to upgrade skills, give information, and recognize credentials in order to obtain access to the global labor market and boost productivity in both the organized and unorganized sectors. The purpose of this study was to gain an understanding of India's current skill development policy initiatives and to identify strategies for producing world-class training for people locally through the effective utilization of GoI skill development schemes. Primary data was gathered through personal interviews with government officials and training providers, while secondary data was extracted from government documents, portals, case studies, research papers, and the International Labour Organization's (ILO) and World Bank's (WB) websites, respectively. The study's findings indicate that India is well-positioned to benefit from the demographic dividend by providing a trained workforce to meet the global and domestic demand for skilled labor. To address this, the Government of India launched a National Policy on Skill Development, with the goal of giving required skills training to 500 million individuals by 2022. However, there are various obstacles, such as training quality, curriculum consistency, and global recognition of courses. Adopting a strong approach is necessary for the country to establish a framework for quality skills, education and training. The formation of Skill Development Universities in each state will address the global standard requirements for academic program creation, evaluation, and certification. Private participation in infrastructure construction and participant training will be more appropriate.

The study was conducted by **Chavda and Trivedi (2015)** and was named "Impact of Age on Skill Development in Different Groups of Students." The primary objective was to determine the effect of age on skill development among students of various ages. Additionally, it sought to examine the effect of gender on students' skill development. To accomplish these goals, the Walker's Life Skills Test (2009) was employed, which assesses four distinct categories of life skills: (1) social etiquette, (2) communication, (3) self-esteem, and (4) hygiene. A random sample of 150 students aged 11 to 13 years, 14 to 17 years, and 18 to 20 years was drawn from schools and colleges in Ahmadabad city. The study's findings indicated that pupils aged 14-17 years developed their skills more rapidly than those aged 11-13 years and 18-20 years. However, the study discovered no statistically significant difference between boys and girls when all age groups are considered. Thus, the study showed that age and maturity, rather than gender, are the most important factors in skill development.

Amandeep (2015) examined the state of skills and education in India in his paper, "Skill Development in Higher Education: Trends and Issues." According to the report, India is ranked seventh globally in the fields of accounting and finance personnel, information technology personnel, secretaries, personal assistants, receptionists, administrative assistants and office support personnel, teachers, engineers, marketing/public relations/ communications personnel, sales managers, management/executive legal personnel, and researchers. While the number of colleges has increased, there is still a significant gap, necessitating the need for skill development programs. This has to be expanded across several sectors, with a stronger emphasis on private partnership skill development programs.

Kanchan and Sakshi (2015) published research titled "Indian skill development efforts and strategies." The study's aims were to ascertain the state, problems, and impact of skill development efforts and strategies in India, for which data was gathered from secondary sources such as journals, magazines, articles, and media reports, among others. According to the study's findings, around 80% of India's workforce, whether rural and urban, lacks recognizable and marketable skills. Thus, the study concluded that by closing this gap through various skill development initiatives, India might position itself as a worldwide powerhouse for qualified manpower.

Abhishek and Aditya (2015) carried out an evaluation of "Skill Development Programs: A Project Management Perspective." The objectives were to study the difficulties associated with implementing a skill development program and, as a result, to evaluate the present model of skill training, development, and placement. Secondary data was gathered from public sources, while data from the parent firm, Infrastructure Leasing & Financial Services (IL & FS), was received with mutual consent for scholarly reasons. The study's findings indicate that the government's primary problem in launching skill development programs in India is securing appropriate financing to support existing skill development projects. As a result, adopting a bottom-up pyramid approach is critical, as skills comprise a significant portion of the capability of the skills. Additionally, the analysis discovered a significant gender imbalance in enrollment in skill development courses and streams. The solution is for NGOs and Panchyats to educate women and their families about Vocational Educational Training (VET) and to assist current female applicants in forming self-help groups.

Mehdi and Chaudhry (2015) emphasized India's demographic dividend, which policymakers can use for economic development, in their research paper on the potential of human capital in India's future workforce. The study asserts that policymakers must capitalize on this vast human capital. They must meet the needs of the industry, which should be the primary emphasis of skills initiatives. Thus, skill development refers to the process of equipping trainees with the necessary fundamental competencies to secure meaningful employment. Thus, the knowledge economy's requirements must be met concurrently with industrial requirements through investments in health and education that should flow down to the local level.

Kaptan (2014) stressed the critical function and necessity of skill development and capacity building programs in the nation's growth through our education system in his paper titled "Skill Development and Capacity Building- Role of Education Institutions." It emphasized the importance of aligning the current educational system with industrial requirements and labor market demands, which can be accomplished through increasing the quality and productivity of the labor force through skill development programs. Additionally, the study revealed that there is a critical need for capacity building and skill development programs that involve educational institutions' active engagement and engagement.

Bhiwa (2014) discovered that, notwithstanding India's illustrious participation in the G20, our human development index, HDI, remains dismally low and requires massive government engagement and initiatives. Our education expenditure is 3.4 percent of GDP, which is extremely low compared to other countries, such as Thailand, which spent 7.6 percent of GDP on education (in the year 2014). India's population share of the globe is 17.6 percent, and it has the highest proportion of working-age people, providing a chance to achieve inclusiveness and productivity through investing in education and developing the technical skills, soft skills, and industrial knowledge of the Indian youth. The government has taken several measures to encourage skill development programs in various areas, including the establishment of the National Skill Development Council and the National Knowledge Commission.

Kapur (2014) attempted to explore the topic of skill development in India in his paper titled "Skills Development in India." Additionally, it aimed to examine the initiatives and policies that have been launched in this approach. The study highlighted a variety of programs and policies, educational and training institutions, and skill development centers that have been built in India to assist in skill development. It demonstrates that rural populations are still extremely backwards and require suitable training to become self-sufficient in resource usage, governance, and leadership. Thus, numerous training facilities have been established in both urban and rural areas to impart skill development activities such as literacy skills (3 Rs, i.e. reading, writing, and arithmetic), computer skills, artisan skills, production, and manufacturing, among others. This will aid individuals tremendously in the long term in developing independent thinking and self-reliance.

The India Skill Report (2014) cited skilled laborers' underachieved status in India. It concluded that if we continue at our current rate of skill development, India's industrial sector will face a 75-80% skill gap. There will be an abundance of human resources in the country, but they will be lacking in smart hands and heads that firms require, as well as occupations for which the perfect fit is unavailable. The economic consequences of this vicious cycle are quantifiable, but the social cost of a powerhouse of educated but dissatisfied millennials who are directionless and jobless is unfathomable.

Raina (2013) undertook the study, titled "Skilling Initiative for Undergraduate Students at the Entry Level: A Case Study," to examine how an undergraduate college attempts to bridge skill gaps using feedback mechanisms. The study examined how education and skill development are critical components of a country's success. Additionally, it emphasized the relevance and necessity of undergraduate skill development activities in bridging skill gaps. The study found that efforts should be made to shift the system from its current model of education to one that is developmental in nature and is integrated with market needs and opportunities.

Mohanraj (2013) in his research discussed the changes that are happening in the Indian informal employment market. The study has mentioned that this sector plays an important role as it contributes 85% of the workforce of the country. A gap between formal and informal sector employment opportunities always exists. If we compare the absorption of human resources, then the formal sector does not have the capacity to recruit a major part of the workforce as it requires specific skills. But the unorganized sector is plagued by very low wages which is insufficient to provide the basic needs of the workforce. Working conditions too are unsafe and there is an overall lack of basic facilities at the worksite. To improve this condition, they need proper training and proper development of their skills. Without the skills they cannot overcome their problems. Government has taken so many initiatives in recent years to provide them proper training. But the training needed is even bigger. It should cover a larger target by which the informal sector can act as an employment contributor and social benefactor.

Mehrotra et al. (2013) in their paper mentioned that the skill gap among the workforce is a serious issue and this needs to be addressed on an urgent basis. In this paper the authors defined a skilled workforce as those who have either vocational training or government certified skills. Initially, to identify the skill enhancement programmes, the government developed sector skills councils to identify the core areas where the skill gap is wider. This is the first stage that enables to generate huge untapped areas where workers can be absorbed provided, they have the required skills. Subsequently the concept of re – skilling emerged. Again, the gap was wider as most of the skill sets are learned through practice without taking the help of any formal training.

Bello et al (2013) research emphasized the importance of ICT in vocational and technical education. According to them, there is a need to focus on the workforce's employability because they lack skills and traditional employment programs are insufficient to meet demand and industry requirements. This has grown much more critical as technology advances. The workforce in this country is not familiar with the ICT technologies used in modern businesses. This has prompted the expansion of ICT-enabled training in the knowledge-based economy.

National Planning Commission (2013) in the report also emphasized upon the implementation of the skill enhancement program in India and also discussed the various strategic frameworks in this direction. Special emphasis had been given in the 12th five-year plan (2012- 2017) to different skill-oriented courses in higher levels of education. The main objective of this plan was to bring the employment scenario up by generating new work opportunities. It will also help to exceed the projected number of the labour force. There is a need to add dimensions in the skill enhancement program. Along with increased skills, there is a need to implement social security features, adequate working hours etc. in the existing employment system. The 12th Five Year Plan also included the objective to change the underemployment situation to a full employment situation. If there is a shift from low wages to higher wage brackets, then this objective may be achievable leading to the overall growth of the economy.

Venkatanarayana & Mahendra (2012) in the study enumerated the development of the workforce in India by analyzing the data from Census 2011. It has been observed in the study that there is a fast slowdown of development in the overall labor force, especially among the female workers, between the years 2001 and 2011. In spite of all the efforts, the growth rate of employment has decreased in the last decade. Mobility of labour is crucial in the knowledge-based economy. Therefore, the economy has also become demanding for more skilled labour. The theoretical background of labour force movement suggests that the excess labour in the agricultural sector will move to the industrial or manufacturing sector till the time the wage differences remain. As a result of this, most of the employees who are working in the agricultural sector failed to secure a job in the formal sector.

Okada (2012) in the study, titled "Skills Development for Youth in India: Problems and Opportunities," addressed the educational and job opportunities available to Indian youths, as well as the challenges associated with skill development. According to the report, in order to enjoy the demographic dividend, the government of India should start on an ambitious route of talent development in order to close the enormous skills gap and align it with industrial requirements. For more than half a century, both within and outside the formal school system, well-institutionalized public vocational education and training systems have existed. However, they are insufficiently large to handle a huge number of school graduates, and they have failed to educate young people with the practical skills that the industry wants to have. As a result, youth access to vocational training is limited. To meet this demand, the government of India has stepped up its efforts to increase the number of skilled people. It has designed a National Skills Development Policy and a National Manufacturing Policy; established a new institutional framework for accelerating and coordinating skills development initiatives; and created the National Vocational Education Qualification Framework (NVEQF). Training institutes now have increased autonomy and involvement in the private sector, as well as enhanced governance and curriculum.

In the research paper, **Hajela (2012)** discussed the problems associated with lack of skilled workforce. Since the informal sector constitutes a huge segment of the workforce, adequate training arrangement for them is absolutely necessary to run the business smoothly. But most of the time this has been ignored. Even the vocational training programmes run by the government are not adequate to provide skill-based training to the workers of these informal sectors. In some cases, on the job training is adopted but the mechanism is not full proof. As a result, the entire system actually works in reverse direction.

UNICEF's 2012 report contains a thorough examination of the "global evaluation of life skills education programs." The report's objective was to examine life skills education initiatives and evaluate their efficacy, efficiency, and sustainability. "UNICEF has long advocated for life skills education and has provided assistance to a number of countries. "Life skills education has been identified as a critical component in preparing young people to face challenges and hazards. The objectives of life-skill education need the development of a comprehensive curriculum that encompasses not just information and skills, but also conduct and values. Life skills education should be integrated into the school curriculum, it is advised. Additionally, it has been suggested that UNICEF provides clear guidelines for assessing life skills education in order to facilitate the integration of effective life skills education into the educational system.

Chenoy (2012) said in his research that the government's primary objective should be to increase labor efficiency, which may be accomplished through liberalization. However, this requires leveraging both social capital and the economy's resource base. Thus, greater emphasis should be placed on training and skill development of the labor force in order to foster economic development. According to Chenoy, "annual enrollment in vocational courses in India is approximately 5.5 million, compared to 90 million in China and 11.3 million in the United States."

Yasar et al. (2011) investigated the informal learning potential of social media. It has been asserted that interaction with people and technology boosts people's knowledge. Informal learning is frequently referred to as interacting with a coworker, watching a television show, or surfing the internet. It can be defined as the most effective method of knowledge acquisition since it improves a person's desire to learn and self-motivation. Individuals can create personal pages on several social networking sites and connect with friends to share information. There are numerous types of social media, including blogs, microblogging, wikis, podcasts, and forums. It is also evaluated as a beneficial tool for informal learning in the workplace. There is a fundamental distinction between informal and non-formal learning. Non-formal education is mostly curriculum-based, whereas informal education is based on social media and requires technology proficiency.

Tas (2011) demonstrated the critical nature of information and communication technology education for development through a case study. The author argues that it is critical for groups of people who are socioeconomically disadvantaged and necessary for poverty alleviation. The majority of people are having difficulty finding work due to a lack of ICT knowledge and experience. It has been suggested that peer to peer training be used as the mode of instruction. This way, individuals can improve their technical ability, presenting ability, communication ability, and verbal ability. The moment has already come when basic IT training is required for any profession. As a result, IT education plays a critical role in the advancement and well-being of individuals and communities.

Majumdar (2008) focused his research on workforce development issues, practices, challenges, and policy directions in India, particularly the need to reposition technical and vocational education and training (TVET) for the development of high-quality skilled workers and knowledge workers while also facilitating the process of incorporating the unorganized and informal sector. Establishing relationships with industry and creating options for vertical mobility for Vocational Stream graduates.

Adams (2007) has reviewed the contribution of skill development of the youth in transition to work. There are some factors which can influence workforce development. Apprenticeship, work experience, education level, different labour market programmes are considered as those factors. These kinds of non-formal training programmes make possible the operation of the labour market. Labour market policies influence the job creation for youth. A new set of challenges can be seen for skill development and sustainable developments while the movement from schools into the workforce. It has been suggested that there should be intervention of public authority, public financing of private providers and training from the enterprises to solve all these issues.

Richardson & Teese (2007) has addressed the issue of skill shortages and its negative impact on the economy. He defines skill shortage as a condition where a worker is not able to earn the market wage rate. It is a proven fact that employers are always looking for different qualities but having all the qualities under one workforce is not possible though not impossible. Certain skills are general in nature and certain skills need specialized and technical knowledge. For the second case, the existing system is not able to generate adequate manpower. As a result of which the skill gap widens.

Chand, Srivastava & Singh (2017) discussed the role of ICT to provide adequate facilities to rural workforces who are mostly deprived of these facilities. It is noticed most of the time; these people are not getting information about government facilities or benefits. The use of ICT tools can help the rural people in building networks for communication, empowerment, which will increase their participation in the sphere of employment and skills. Creation of facilities is not adequate unless sufficient training is provided to these needy sections of the society.

Matthews (2007) emphasized the increasing importance of ICT-based skill upgrading training in bridging the demand-supply gap for workers sought by industry. The majority of Asian countries have seen rapid growth in ICT, which is a positive sign. Initially, growth was limited to metropolitan regions, but gradually, the system expanded into rural areas, creating new business potential. This ready-made market has become the primary draw for the majority of marketers. However, it is clear that simply having clients and the essential workers in the new market would not be enough unless further investment is made in the rural regions to construct the necessary infrastructure. The industry's requirements are changing, and in light of these changes, existing technology-enabled services should be utilised to enhance workers' capability and adaptability. Skill enhancement should be done in accordance with industrial requirements, and priorities should be established for "developing a skill enhancement system that is technologically integrated.

The UNDP's Human Development Report (2003) noted the likely positive effects of ICT on the rural poor's lives. The government and them are most concerned with those who live below the poverty line. Additionally, they are frequently excluded from government-funded programs due to a lack of understanding. Occasionally, the procedures for acquiring facilities are unknown. The proliferation of benefits earmarked for the rural poor aggravates the situation. Providing basic amenities and services necessary for survival is a difficult endeavor. Over time, it has become critical to provide enough social security for those who fall into this vulnerable category. ICT offers the advantage of offering ground-level services. On the one hand, it has the potential to educate and train the workforce, while also delivering additional value-added services such as financial services and government benefits. The issue is one of adoption of these technology-enabled services. The facilities are available, but to make them a reality, all stakeholders must collaborate. The primary purpose should be to raise awareness.

2.3 Summary & Scope of Literature Review

From the above detailed review of literature studies, it can be summed that youth mobilization to get trained is necessary in the skilling exercise to capitalize on India's demographic dividend leading to economic and sustainable development of the economy. There is an imminent concern to curb mass migration and empower the youth through skill enhancement using the ICT and latest technology. Scaling up aspirations for current occupations, as well as attracting the correct training partners and managing stakeholders effectively, all require due consideration in skilling ecosystems. The implementing agencies and training partners must consider and properly monitor the implementation of 'inclusion' principles for women, minorities, and individuals with special needs in a gradual way. More importantly, the classification of skilled, semi-skilled, and unskilled people must be consistent with the National Skill Qualification Framework's skill levels (NSQF). All this will pave the path for skilling India endeavor in the right perspective. The scope of the literature review has been comprehensive in addressing pertinent studies in these areas, which is represented in the figure 2.1 below: -

Figure 2.1: Scope and extent of ROL studies

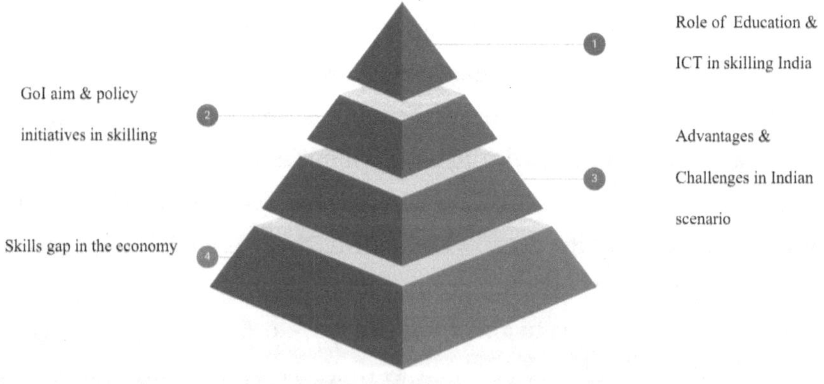

- Skills gap in the economy
- Advantages & Challenges in Indian scenario
- GoI aim & policy initiatives in skilling
- Role of Education & ICT in skilling India

2.4 Research gaps addressed

Drawing from the above scope and coverage of the review of literature, it can be inferred that most of the studies and reports have pointed the importance of the skiing the workforce, the skill gap prevalent in the economy, the negative impact of this on the economy, the GoI policy initiatives and aim in skilling India. Besides, studies have focused on the formal and informal sectors and the problems faced by them besides the role of education, allied institutions and ICT in uplifting the skills and employability. While also advocating the inclusion prerogative of the GoI. But there is hardly any study that has been conducted to examine the PMKVY as perceived by the youth trainees, especially in Haryana. PMKVY 2 (2016-20) is a recent flagship program for skilling the youths, (i.e., through STT and RPL). So, this study fills a critical research void and paves the path for the proper implementation of the PMKVY in other parts of the country.

2.5 Conclusion

This chapter has offered an exhaustive overview of the available literature over the last 15 years in a methodical manner, emphasizing the research issues and laying the groundwork for this study as well. The following chapter goes over the research methodology used in this study.

Chapter 3

Methodlogies Used

3.1 Introduction

This chapter describes the research methodology related to the study. It entails extensive elaboration on the research process and the steps involved to conduct the research process of the study in a systematic manner. Next, the objectives are elucidated in conjunction with the hypotheses that were developed for the study. Henceforth, the research methodology is presented entailing the research design, sampling methodology, data collection methodology, reliability and validity, statistical techniques for analysis, ethical considerations and limitations of the study.

3.2 Research Process

The term "research" refers to a systematic search for knowledge. "Research entails defining and redefining problems, formulating hypotheses or suggested solutions; collecting, organising, and evaluating data; making deductions and reaching conclusions; and, finally, carefully testing the conclusions to see if they fit the formulating hypothesis," according to Clifford Woody (1927).

"Creative and systematic work undertaken to increase the stock of knowledge, including knowledge of humans, culture, and society, and the use of this stock of knowledge to devise new applications" is defined as "creative and systematic work undertaken to increase the stock of knowledge, including knowledge of humans, culture, and society, and the use of this stock of knowledge to devise new applications." It's used to establish or confirm facts, reinforce earlier work's findings, solve new or existing issues, prove theorems, and generate new theories.

"The research process consists of a sequence of procedures that must be followed in order to properly conduct research and arrive at the desired study results/outcomes."

The research steps as adopted in this study are represented in figure 3. 1 which entails the main steps as: -

3.2.1 Formulating the Research Problem

The first step in the research process is to formulate a research problem. These two steps can be used to determine research problems based on the relationship between the variables:

- First, a thorough understanding of the research problem
- Second, redefining research problems and making it coherent with research investigation and data analysis.

3.2.2 Literature Review & Hypotheses Development

The extensive literature review in the research domain by eminent researchers that will form the backbone of the study. This conforms to comprehending the research studies, assimilating, organizing and summarizing the extant literature to assess the nature of the problem, identify the research gaps and scope of the study.

After a literature review, the next step is hypothesis development in a precise and specific manner. These are the preliminary assumptions that are supported through the literature review studies and further taken up for testing and validation to arrive at the objectives of the study.

3.2.3 Research Design

The primary goal of study design is to "get significant facts and data with the least amount of time, effort, and money." The following are the several types of research designs:

1. Exploration research design
2. Description research design
3. Causal research design
4. Experimentation research design

It is imperative to narrow down on a specific research design in accordance with study objectives that in turn, provides a holistic outlook of the research study.

3.2.4 Sampling Methodology

Once the research design has been decided, the next stage leads to sampling methodology. In this case, first the appropriate sample design is finalized before initiating data collection from the given sample size. This pertains to choosing either "Probability or Non-probability Sampling techniques" for the study. When each independent element of a sample has an equal chance of selection, it is known as 'Probability Sampling', while on the other hand, if selection of samples is being influenced by some judgment, then such technique is referred to as "Non-probability sampling".

3.2.5 Data Collection and Analysis

Data collection refers to the gathering of information from a sample, which can be divided into primary and secondary data. Primary data is obtained through a direct survey or experiment, whereas secondary data is obtained from journals, academic literature, previous studies, industry reports, and other sources.

3.2.6 Interpretation of Results and Presentation

For a researcher to take a broader view of the problem statement or prepare a concept or a model, the hypothesis needs to be tested and accepted. In fact, the actual ability of research is to arrive at a significant overview of the research problem, enabling the results to be inferred into specific reports after detailed analysis of the drawn results.

The steps in the research process, as used in this study also, have been outlined in the figure 3.1

Figure 3.1: Steps in the research process

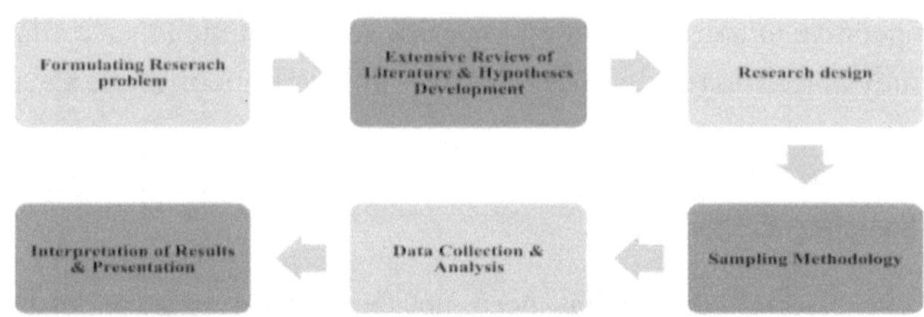

Taking it further, we present the Research Objectives and the Hypotheses developed in this context (Section 3.3), followed by discussion of the Research Design and methodology adopted to arrive at the study outcomes (Section 3.4).

3.3 Research Objectives & Hypotheses

3.3.1 Objectives of study

The main purpose of this study is to conduct a comprehensive evaluation of the PMKVY Training from the youth's perspective in select districts of Haryana.

The primary objectives of this study are stated as follows: -

- To understand the demographic profile of beneficiaries under the PMKVY scheme in select districts of Haryana.
- To understand the awareness and its association with participation of the trainee youth / beneficiaries in Kaushal Melas with respect to PMKVY training.
- To understand the beneficiary's Aspirations for the training sector and Training imparted under PMKVY.
- To understand the sub-components in the delivery mechanisms of PMKVY Training.

- To identify and validate the beneficiary's perceptions on the components of PMKVY Training
- To understand the relationship of the components of PMKVY Training with effectiveness of PMKVY Training (in terms of skills enhancement, satisfaction and standard of living)

3.3.2 Hypotheses of the Study

Objective 2: To understand the awareness and its association with participation of the trainee youth / beneficiaries in Kaushal Melas with respect to PMKVY training.

Table 3.1: Hypotheses w.r.t. Objective 2

Association between Beneficiary's Participation in Kaushal Melas and their Awareness PMKVY Trainings
Hypotheses
H1: There is no significant association between beneficiary's awareness on the Training Sector of Interest with their participation in Kaushal Mela under PMKVY.
H2: There is no significant association between beneficiary's awareness on eligibility criteria for the enrollment in PMKVY training with their participation in Kaushal Mela under PMKVY.
H3: There is no significant association between beneficiary's awareness on availability of the training centers in the district with their participation in Kaushal Mela under PMKVY.
H4: There is no significant association between beneficiary's awareness that PMKVY training is free with their participation in Kaushal Mela under PMKVY.

Objective 6: To understand the relationship of the components of PMKVY Training with effectiveness of PMKVY Trainings (in terms of skills enhancement, satisfaction and standard of living)

Table 3.2: Hypotheses w.r.t. Objective 6

Relationship between components of PMKVY Trainings and Effectiveness of PMKVY
H5: There is no significant relationship between Training Quality and skill enhancement of PMKVY
H6: There is no significant relationship between Resources and Support and skill enhancement of PMKVY
H7: There is no significant relationship between Infrastructure and skill enhancement of PMKVY
H8: There is no significant relationship between Training Quality and Satisfaction of Beneficiaries
H9: There is no significant relationship between Resources & Support and Satisfaction of Beneficiaries
H10: There is no significant relationship between Infrastructure and Satisfaction of Beneficiaries
H11: There is no significant relationship between Training Quality and Standard of Living of Beneficiaries
H12: There is no significant relationship between Resources and Support and Standard of Living of Beneficiaries
H13: There is no significant relationship between Infrastructure and Standard of Living of Beneficiaries

3.3.3 Research Model

The research models for the above-mentioned hypotheses are represented in the figure given below: -

Figure 3.2: Hypothesized models
Model 1

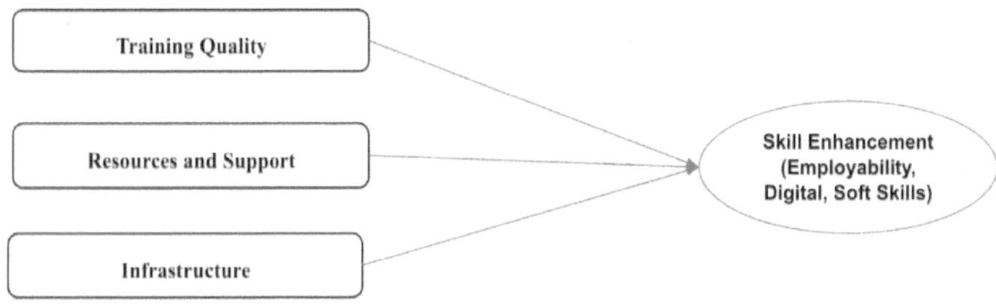

Model 2

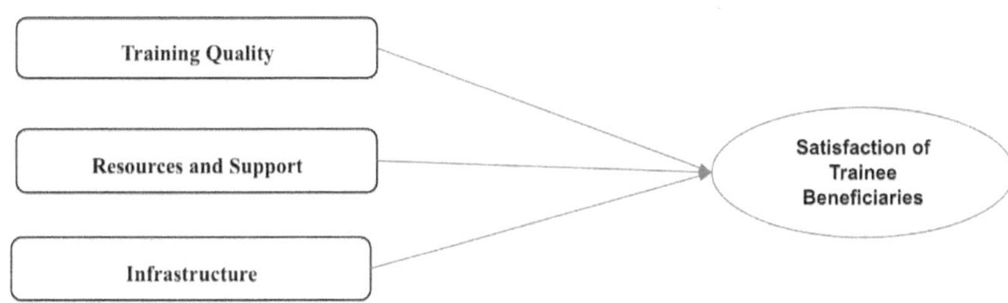

Model 3

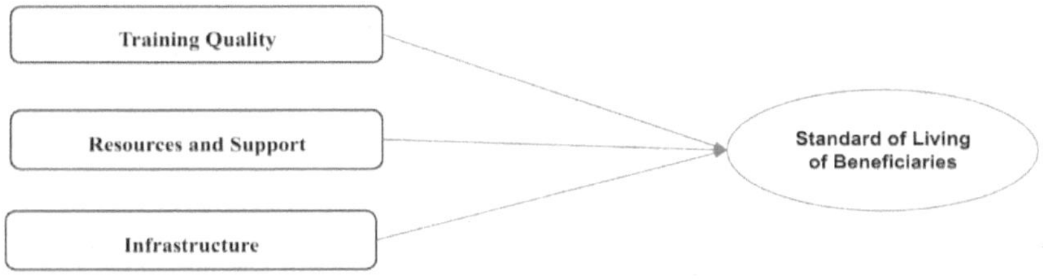

3.4 Research Design and Methodology

3.4.1 Research Design

The framework or plan for performing a market research project is known as research design (Malhotra & Dash, 2013). It lays the groundwork for the research to be carried out. The research design could be exploratory, descriptive, or casual, depending on the nature of the study's problem.

Exploratory research

Exploratory research is used to identify and explain the nature of a problem, as well as to gain a deeper understanding of the situation for the researcher. It allows the researcher to gain a deeper understanding of the issue. "The objective of exploratory research," according to Zikmund (2000), "includes diagnosing a situation, screening alternatives, and discovering new ideas."

Descriptive research

According to Zikmund (2000), "When the problem is structured, descriptive research is used." It addresses the questions of who, where, what, how, and when. It's used to emphasise the uniqueness of a group or an observable event.

Causal research

"Problems are structured in causal research as well. Causal research focuses on determining the cause-and-effect links between the study's stated variables." Malhotra and Dash (Malhotra & Dash, 2013). The goal is to separate cause and effect and investigate the existence and scope of cause-effect interactions between variables.

The current study will use a 'descriptive' research approach to give a detailed evaluation of the PMKVY programme in a few Haryana districts. This research will use a descriptive research design (cross-sectional study design frame at one specific time period) with self-administered questionnaires to the trainees in the PMKVY affiliate training centres.

3.4.2 Sampling Methodology

3.4.2.1 Sampling Frame

The representation of the elements of the target population is known as the sampling frame. The sampling frame for this study would be trainee/ youth beneficiaries under the PMKVY (2016-20) from 13 Haryana districts spanning rural, semi-urban, and urban regions. As a result, the current study generalises the findings of PMKVY youth beneficiaries who were trained at PMKVY-affiliated Training Centers in Haryana. The basic reasons for choosing Haryana were that it qualifies on the grounds on: -

❖ Rapid Industrialization- so, there is abundant provision of skilled workforce that needs to be harnessed according to the current pace of industrialization and transformation to make them employable. The geographical proximity of Haryana with Delhi/NCR as industrial hubs is another big economic advantage accruing to it.

❖ Increase in population – a trend which is observable in the recent years and so the challenge lies in making them skilled and employable.

❖ Shrinking land bank due to decrease in the Agriculture Sector- as there has been a shift in people's mindset towards jobs and they have moved away from core agriculture

❖ Recognition of prior learning, RPL- which is also another thrust area under the PMKVY along with short term training, STT and which targets the existing workforce with some experience (that is available here). As a result, the RPL strives to align the skills of the country's unregulated workforce with the NSQF requirements.

3.4.2.2 Sampling Method

The sampling methodology can be classified into two categories, as: -

- Probability Sampling Method
- Non probability Sampling Method

Each person in the population has a known non-zero chance of being chosen in ***probability sampling***. Stratified sampling, systematic sampling, and random sample are some of the approaches used.

Members of the population are selected in a non-random manner in ***non-probability sampling***. Quota sampling, convenience sampling, judgement sampling, and snowball sampling are just a few examples.

The stratified random selection strategy was judged to be suitable for the research objective after examining the practicality of data collection and response generation against the enrolled participants. When subpopulations within a larger population differ, stratified random sampling is justified because it is more efficient to sample each subpopulation separately. Because each district and its associated skill training centres can be considered a separate subgroup in this study, stratified random sampling was used. To decrease response biases and maximise the accuracy and generalizability of the study, a step-by-step procedure (as shown in Figure 3.2) was used to collect responses from a representative and large sample. The following is a list of the sample size selection criteria: -

3.4.2.3 Sample size Selection

Initially, the sample size for the study was taken from 13 districts of Haryana covering 338 skill centers in these districts. The comprehensive list of centers was obtained from the NSDC website. However, all the skill centres were not taken into account and only those centres were selected in the study which were operational and where many beneficiaries were enrolled for the training in different job roles.

Accordingly, the sampling technique and size was determined in 4 steps procedure, as follows -

Figure 3.3: Steps in Sampling Process

In the first place, the 13 districts from Haryana were selected. Then, the minimum sample size was ascertained for each of the districts (using the sample size formula) at 95% C.I. and assuming 0.05 margin of error, as per the defined population.

The sample size formula is represented below. -

$$n = \frac{z^2 \times \hat{p}(1-\hat{p})}{\varepsilon^2}$$

$$n = \frac{1.96^2 \times 0.5(1-0.5)}{0.05^2} = 384.16$$

Once the minimum sample size was ascertained (i.e. 385 for a large population), then the sampling selection criteria was fixed at 10% of the computed sample size from each district skill center. This was done since covering all the skill centres was beyond the scope of the study. However, this proportionality will give a representative sample that encompasses all the districts and the skill centers, and it will also ensure that the sample spread is varied across all the districts covered under the PMKVY in Haryana.

The sample distribution is represented in the next table.

Table 3.3: Sample Distribution

Districts	Skill Centers	Enrolled	Sample Size/10 (As per Stat Formula at 95% CL)	Sample Size Chosen for the Study (105 of the D)
Ambala	16	10132	371	37
Bhiwani	22	25112	379	38
CharkhiDadri	6	577	231	23
Faridabad	23	11400	372	37

Districts	Skill Centers	Enrolled	Sample Size/10 (As per Stat Formula at 95% CL)	Sample Size Chosen for the Study (105 of the D)
Fatehabad	15	16263	376	38
Gurgaon	23	15843	376	38
Hisar	26	26235	379	38
Jhajjar	10	9517	370	37
Jind	20	12868	374	37
Kaithal	13	9391	370	37
Karnal	15	7496	366	37
Kurukshetra	10	18623	377	38
Mahendragarh	17	13238	374	37
Nuh (Mewat)	16	4569	355	36
Palwal	11	2326	330	33
Panchkula	19	6287	363	36
Panipat	13	8161	367	37
Rewari	7	5563	360	36
Rohtak	9	11657	372	37
Sirsa	24	14085	374	37
Sonipat	10	11219	372	37
Yamunanagar	13	11056	372	37
Total	**338**	**251618**	**7980**	**798**

So, the calculated sample size across the 13 districts and various skill centres in the districts arrived at 798. The questionnaire was distributed to 850 respondents, out of which the usable sample was arrived at of 816 respondents. The power of the sample was hereby increased substantially by increasing the minimum sample size requirement of 385 to 816. This will also make the sample more accurate, reliable, and unbiased and reduce error.

3.4.3 Data Collection Methodology

To comprehend the study setting, both primary and secondary sources of data were utilised extensively in this study. The study's primary data gathering method was self-administered questionnaires to Haryana's trainee young recipients. The questionnaire was aimed at ascertaining beneficiary's perceptions regarding the various components of the PMKVY training and the impact of these on their overall skill enhancement, satisfaction and standard of living. The questionnaire copy has been included in the Appendix I.

A questionnaire is described as "a form that comprises a collection of questions and is addressed to a statistically significant number of individuals in order to collect information for a survey" (Tustin et al., 2000). (2005). The questionnaire for this quantitative study included closed–ended, multiple-choice, and Likert-scale questions. It related to questions detailing the demographic information, PMKVY training components and skill enhancement and satisfaction of the beneficiaries.

Secondary data were also useful in forming insight and giving systematic direction to the study. To access the secondary data, the PMKVY dashboards and reports of government and websites, like PMKVY, Haryana skill development mission were extensively utilized. Besides, the studies in this area were also searched online in the research papers from Science direct, Google scholar and SSRN. However, as is the case with secondary data, due care was taken to check its suitability, reliability and authenticity for the study purpose.

3.4.4 Reliability and Validity

3.4.4.1. Reliability

It is very important to ascertain the Reliability and Validity of the questionnaire before proceeding further with data analysis to arrive at the study results.

As per Saunder et al (2009), "there are some threats for reliability that must be captured (like, subject or participant error, subject or participant bias, observer bias and observer error) to increase the accuracy and reliability of the research findings,"

Subject or participant bias: - Such biases develop as a result of the respondent's lack of knowledge or experience. To eliminate bias, respondents were evaluated on their knowledge of the PMKVY programme, and only those trainees who were aware of and enrolled in the PMKVY training were given questionnaires to fill out.

Subject or participant error: - Such errors may occur when respondents are suffering from a physical condition and/or a mental issue of stress at the time of answering the questions. Low response, guessing and answering, or inability to comprehend and grasp the question itself can all result from such circumstances. All efforts were made to make the questions as simple as possible so that they would suit and be simply understood by the respondents.

Observer's bias: - "Observer's bias provides the most serious danger to reliability," according to Saunder et al (2009). It may have a different meaning for the respondent." To eliminate observer bias, the questionnaires were self-administered and required guidance and clarifications at the time of completion. To guarantee that the responses were reliable, the researcher carefully investigated their dependability.

The reliability of the responses was obtained for the Likert-scaled responses using the widely used Cronbach Alpha test, which is used to measure reliability. Cronbach's alpha values greater than.65 were deemed reliable for further study and therapy.

Table 3.4: Reliability of the PMKVY Training Components

Components	Reliability Cronbach Alpha
Training Quality	0.986
Resources and Support	0.921
Infrastructure	0.948

3.4.4.2 Validity

"Validity has to do with the reality of the findings", Saunder et al (2009). "Validity relates to the extent to which the research data and the methods for obtaining the data are accurate, honest and on target," Denscombe, (2009). It implies that the extent to which a study correctly relates to the theme which the researcher intends to measure. For this, the external as well as the internal validity is of prime significance for the study.

External validity pertains to generalization of the results. There are many ways to assess external validity, for example - random sampling.

Internal validity pertains to the design of the study, basically care is taken in carrying out the measurement and decisions on what should be measured or not be measured.

In order to increase the validity of this study, it is based on past studies and the content validity was ascertained by taking feedback from the experts and officials from a few training centres. Moreover, the convergent and discriminant validity was also ascertained through administering the Confirmatory Analysis technique.

Table 3.5: Validity of the PMKVY Training Components

Validity Measures			
PMKVY Training Components	**CR**	**AVE**	**MSV**
1. Infrastructure	0.948	0.697	0.526
2. Training Quality	0.986	0.936	0.532
3. Resources and Support	0.923	0.708	0.532

3.4.5 Techniques for Analysis

The data once collected was in the first place subjected to editing and coding to make it fit for the analysis purpose. Cooper and Schindler (2006) stated "editing is systematic and analytical inspection of completed surveys to check for coherence of data against the criteria/objectives of the study and to check any omissions in the data". Thus, data editing is detection, exclusions, and correction of errors wherever feasible and endorses that highest data quality has been attained.

The collected data was properly checked again for any missing values and then labeled and analysed using the latest statistical software SPSS. To get at the study's aims, statistical procedures involving both descriptive and inferential statistics were used in SPSS.

Descriptive statistics describes data while inferential statistics allows one to draw inferences from that data. Descriptive statistics sums up description in terms of mean, frequency distribution and the mode to gauge mean values and standard deviation and data spread. Inferential statistics are mostly employed in hypothesis testing to get the study's primary conclusions.

The statistical techniques used for data analysis in this study are as: -

3.4.5.1 Chi- Square tests of Association

The Chi-Square Test of Independence analyses whether categorical variables are associated (i.e., whether the variables are independent or related). It's a test that isn't parametric. The Chi-Square Test of Independence is often used to determine whether two or more categorical variables are statistically independent or not.

The Chi-square test of association was used to investigate the relationship between the trainee/youth beneficiary's participation in Kaushal Melas and their understanding of the PMKVY training features in this study. The research issue of whether the Kaushal Melas benefited the learners by enhancing their awareness of the many parts of PMKVY training was answered (like accessibility in their locality, enrollment criterion, etc.).

3.4.5.2. Multiple Regression

Simple linear regression is expanded into multiple regressions. When we wish to anticipate the value of a variable based on the values of two or more other variables, we utilise this method. The dependent variable is the variable we want to forecast (or sometimes, the outcome, target or criterion variable). The independent variables are the factors we use to predict the value of the dependent variable (or sometimes, the predictor, explanatory or regressor variables). Multiple regressions also let you figure out the model's overall fit (variance explained) and the relative contribution of each predictor to the total variance explained.

Stepwise linear regression is a technique for regressing many variables while concurrently eliminating those that aren't significant. Stepwise regression essentially repeats numerous regressions, discarding the weakest associated variable each time. Finally, the variables that best describe the distribution are left. The only criteria are that the data be normally distributed (or, more precisely, that the residuals be) and that the independent variables be uncorrelated (known as co linearity).

The Stepwise linear regression was used in this study to determine the relationship between the three major factors/components of the PMKVY training (i.e. Training Quality, Resources and Support, and Infrastructure Facilities) and trainee satisfaction, standard of living, and skill enhancement as benefit outcomes of undergoing the PMKVY training.

3.4.5.3. Exploratory Factor Analysis (EFA)

It is a technique for data reduction into distinct factors which can then be used for further analysis in a coherent manner. In this study, the technique used for the extraction method was the principal component analysis using promax rotation for identifying the components of the PMKVY training.

3.4.5.4. Confirmatory Factor Analysis (CFA)

The CFA method is used to investigate the link between constructs that has been proposed. A model is built based on the nature of the latent variables or constructs. Various fit statistics in CFA, according to Holtzman and Leich (2014), help to analyse the model fitness for the data. This method aided in the conformance and validation of the constructions (i.e., PMKVY training components).

3.4.6 Ethical Considerations

To begin with the researcher informed the participants on the kind of study that is being undertaken and sought their active cooperation and consent to participate. Leedy and Ormorod, (2005) suggest that- "a consent form which describes the nature of the research project as well as the purpose of one's participation should be shared".

As a result, the participants were informed about the study's goal and were also given an explanation of the study. Furthermore, it was made clear that their participation was entirely optional and that they could opt out of the survey at any time. Only those participants who gave their consent were approached for the survey and due care was taken so that the participants don't feel stressed out. For this reason, the officials at the centre were requested to explain the purpose of the study and its importance to make them at ease and then the researcher was present to fill the questionnaire responses himself after explaining the questions. The confidentiality of the respondents and their trust was gained for using their responses in the right perspective. Thus, this study properly aligns to ethical norms and raises no such concerns from others in this study context.

3.5 Conclusion

To summarise, this chapter presents the research process in a systematic manner in accordance with the study's goals and objectives. The study's sample methodology, data collection methods, and procedures have all been thoroughly discussed. The study's analysis and findings are presented in the next chapter.

Chapter 4

Vignette of Analysis

4.1 Introduction

This chapter provides a thorough assessment of the Pradhan Mantri Kaushal Vikas Yojana, or PMKVY, as it has been implemented in 13 Haryana districts.

All the statistical analyses were conducted at 95% confidence level using the SPSS 25 software. In the first place, the data was set up and tested to check for any outliers and normality distribution, which was found suitable to proceed with further analysis. The analysis along with its interpretation is presented in the following paragraphs: -

4.2. Demographic Profile

The descriptive analysis of frequency and percentage distribution for this is presented in the following tables: -

4.2.1 Gender of the respondents

According to table 4.1, there were 387 male and 429 female respondents among the 816 respondents who took part in this study from Haryana, which is roughly an equal representation.

Table 4.1: Gender of respondents

Gender	Frequency	Percent
Female	429	52.6
Male	387	47.4
Total	**816**	**100**

Figure 4.1: Gender distribution

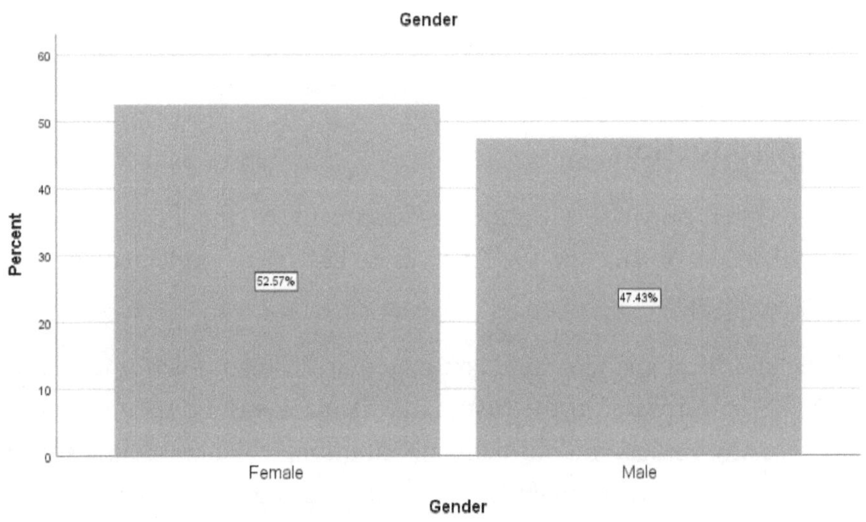

4.2.2 Age Group of the respondents

Table 4.2: Age Group

Age	Frequency	Percent
18 - 24 years	453	55.5
25 - 29 years	363	44.5
Total	**816**	**100**

Figure 4.2: Age Group

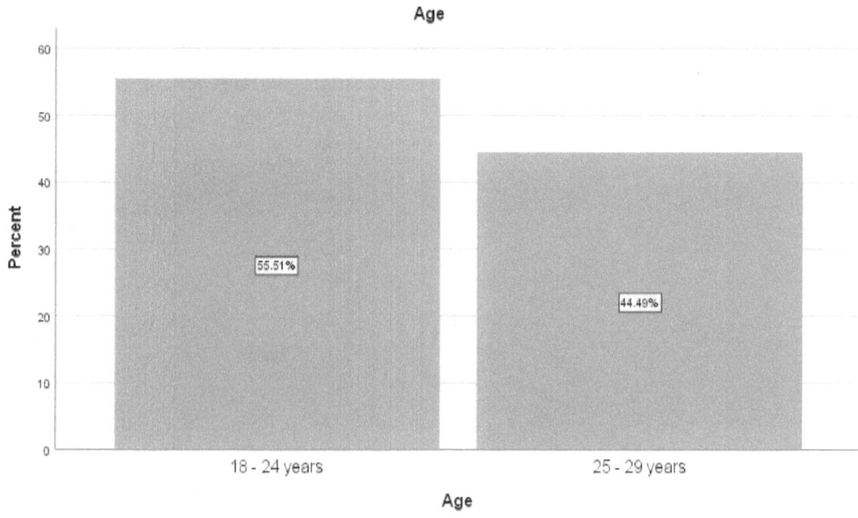

It can be inferred from above that the trainees belonged to 18-24 years (55.5%) and 25-29 years (44.5%) age brackets.

4.2.3 Marital Status of the respondents

Table 4.3: Marital Status

Marital Status	Frequency	Percent
Married	345	42.3
Unmarried	471	57.7
Total	**816**	**100**

Figure 4.3: Marital Status

From the above, it can be inferred regarding the marital status, most of them were unmarried (57.7%), though considerable number of the trainees were married (42.3%)

4.2.4 Education of the respondents

Table 4.4: Education

Education	Frequency	Percent
Primary	10	1.2
10th Pass	218	26.7
Secondary	415	50.9
Graduate	173	21.2
Total	**816**	**100**

Figure 4.4: Education

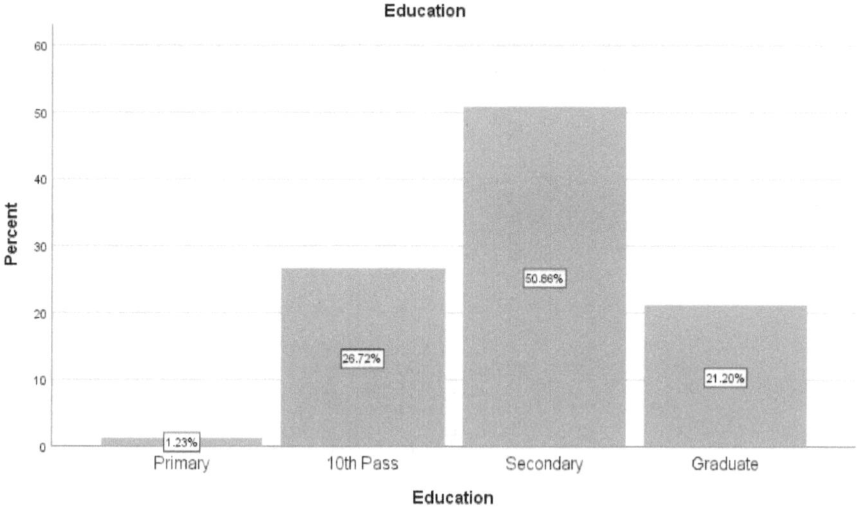

As per the education, it can be inferred that Majority of them were educated, having passed senior secondary level (50.9%), 10th pass (26.7%) and even graduates (21.2%).

4.2.5 Family Size of the respondents

Table 4.5: Family Size

Family Size	Frequency	Percent
1	8	1
2	19	2.3
3	128	15.7
4	333	40.8
5 or More than 5	328	40.2
Total	**816**	**100**

Figure 4.5: Family Size

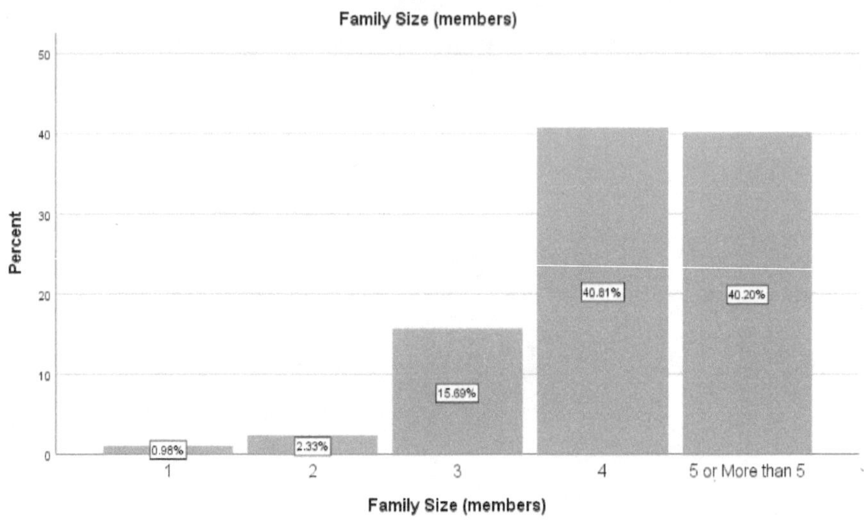

It can be inferred that most of the respondents were hailing from a large joint family with over 4 members (40.8%) or 5 or more family members (40.2%). There were few respondents who were having a nuclear family with 3 members (15.7%) and even less.

4.2.6: Earning Members in the family

Table 4.6: Earning Members in the family

Earning Members in the family		
	Frequency	**Percent**
1	512	62.7
2	197	24.1
3	45	5.5
4	35	4.3
More than 4	27	3.3
Total	**816**	**100**

Figure 4.6: Earning Members in the family

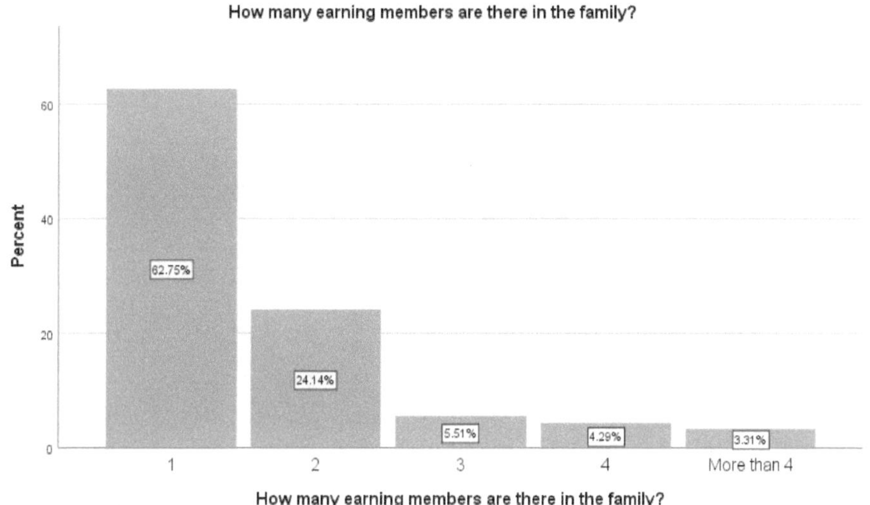

It can be inferred that majority families had a single main earning person (62.7%), followed by 2 earning members in the family (24.1%). However, relatively few respondents belonged to families with 3 or more earning members.

4.2.7: Household Income of the Respondents

Table 4.7: Household Income

Household Income		
	Frequency	**Percent**
Less than Rs.10,000	129	15.8
Rs.10,000 - Rs.20,000	357	43.8
Rs.20,001 - Rs.30,000	204	25
Rs.30,000 - Rs.40,000	110	13.5
More than Rs.40,000	16	2
Total	**816**	**100**

Figure 4.7: Household Income

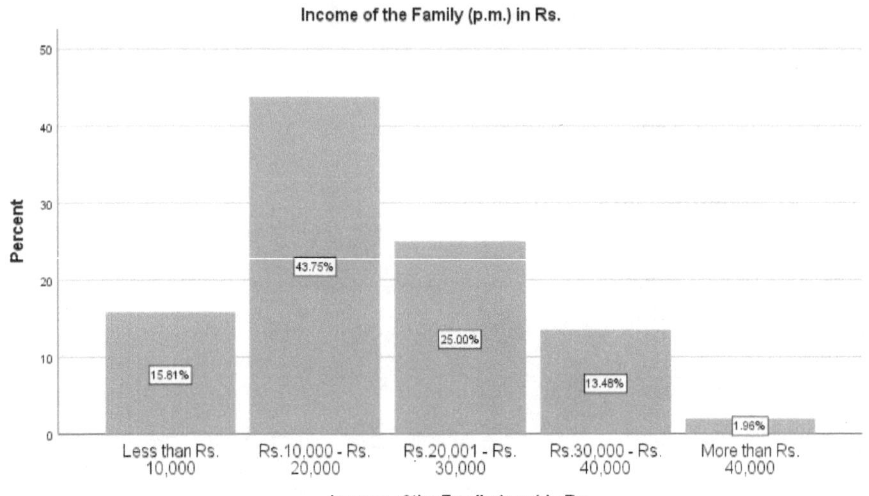

It can be deduced that the respondents' family income ranged from Rs.10,000 to Rs.20,000 (43.8 percent), followed by Rs.20,001-Rs.30,000 (25 percent). There were few responders from the household income groups of less than Rs.10,000 (15.8%) and Rs.30,000 - Rs.40,000 (15.8%). (13.5 percent).

4.2.8: Personal Income of the respondents

Table 4.8: Personal Income

Personal Income		
	Frequency	**Percent**
Nil	601	73.7
Less than Rs.5,000	109	13.4
Less than Rs.10,000	106	13
Total	**816**	**100**

Figure 4.8: Personal Income

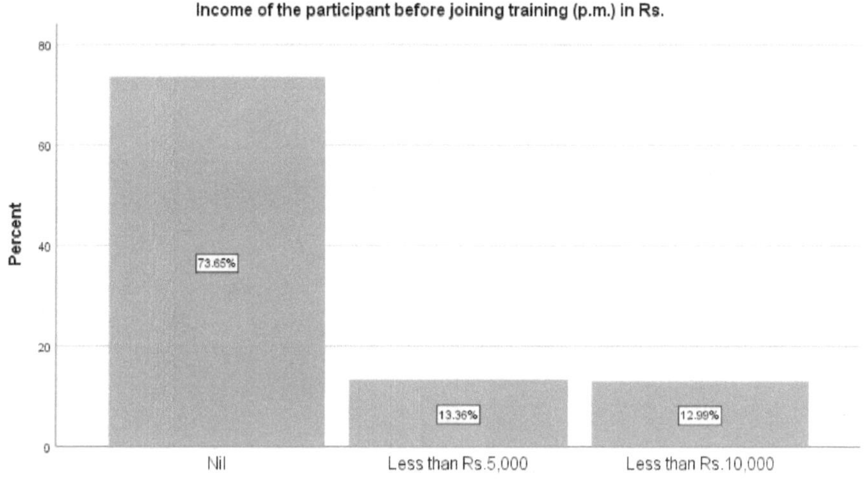

As per the personal income of the respondents, it can be inferred that it was less than Rs 5,000/- (13.4%) and less than Rs.10,000 (13%).

4.2.9: Disability, if any

Table 4.9: Disability

Disability		
	Frequency	**Percent**
Yes	149	18.3
No	667	81.7
Total	**816**	**100**

Figure 4.9: Disability

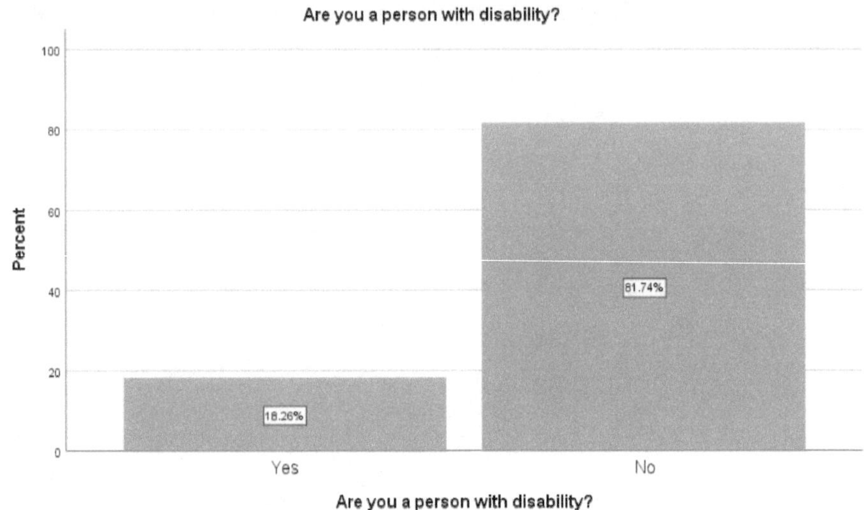

It may be deduced that the majority of the respondents (81.7%) did not have any physical disabilities, while the remaining 18.3 percent did.

4.2.10: Occupation (Before Training) of the Respondents

Table 4.10: Occupation (Before Training)

Occupation Before Training		
	Frequency	**Percent**
Self-employed	99	12.1
Wage Employment	78	9.6
Unemployed	639	78.3
Total	**816**	**100**

Figure 4.10: Occupation (Before Training)

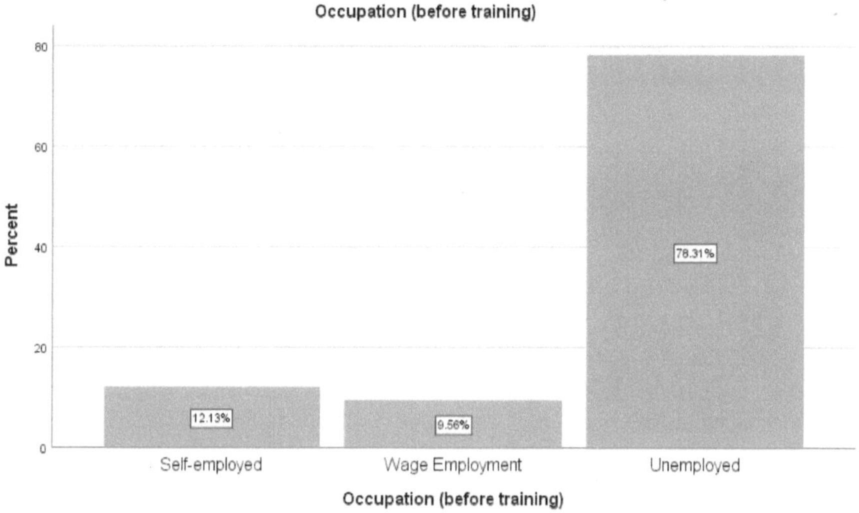

As per the Occupation **(Before Training)** of the respondents, it can be inferred that most were unemployed (78.3%), relatively few respondents were in employment, either self-employed (12.1%) or Wage employment (9.6%).

4.3: Awareness of the PMKVY Training

It's also important to learn about the youth's understanding of PMKVY training components, such as the areas in which training is provided and the eligibility criteria for enrolling in PMKVY training, availability of training centres in their districts, and free-of-cost training. The analysis on these aspects is presented in each of the following subsections, as The table presenting the youth's awareness on the PMKVY training aspects is presented in the table below:

Table 4.11: Awareness on PMKVY Training

Awareness of PMKVY	Yes (%)	No (%)
Training Imparted in the sector of interest	98.4	1.6
Eligibility Criterion for the Enrollment	95.8	4.2
Location of Training Centres	91.1	5.8
Free Training	98.4	1.6

Figure 4.11: Awareness on PMKVY Training

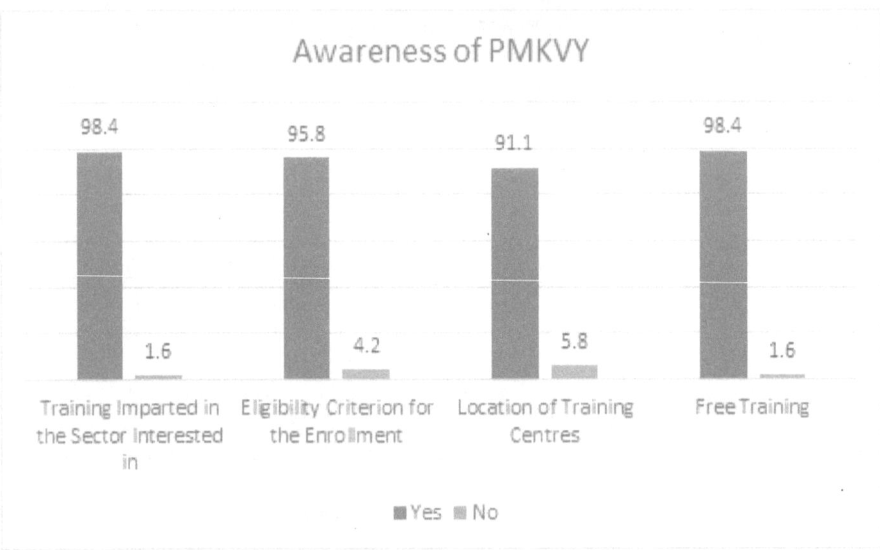

It may be deduced that the vast majority of respondents (98.4%) were aware that training is provided in the field of their choice. It's also safe to assume that the vast majority of responders (95.8%) were aware of the PMKVY training's eligibility requirements. It can be assumed that 91.1 percent of respondents were aware of the training or skill center's location in their district or block. About 3.2 percent said there isn't a training centre in the area. It can be assumed that the vast majority of respondents (98.4%) were aware that the PMKVY course was provided free of charge.

Overall, it can be concluded that the trainees have a high degree of awareness of the PMKVY in their district, which is a highly optimistic indicator for motivating them to participate in training.

4.3.1 Association between Beneficiary's Participation in Kaushal Melas and their Awareness PMKVY Training

Any intervention's success is determined by the youth's willingness to participate in it. This can be accomplished by mobilising and motivating a huge number of young people to engage in the 'Kaushal Melas.' As a result, the youth were first assessed for their understanding of the various parts of PMKVY training, and then the hypothesis was examined to see if there was a link between their involvement in Kaushal Melas and their understanding of PMKVY training aspects. The 'Chi-Square' tests of association were used, with the Independent Variable being 'Participation in the Kaushal Melas,' and the Dependent Variable being 'Awareness of the various parts of the PMKVY training.'

It can be deduced that the kids were well-informed about the many parts of the PMKVY course. In addition, the Chi-square test and cross tabulation findings are presented in summary table 4.12 as follows:

Table 4.12: Chi-Square of Participation in Kaushal Melas and Awareness of PMKVY Training aspects

Awareness of Participants who attended Kaushal Melas	Yes	No	Pearson Chi-Square	df	Asymptotic Significance (2-sided)
Awareness Regarding training is imparted in the sector/industry the respondent is interested in	454	4	12.45	1	0.03
	99.10%	0.90%			
Awareness of eligibility criterion for the enrollment of the training	451	7	18.197	1	0
	98.50%	1.50%			
Awareness of Location of training centers in district/ block	424	23	13.269	2	0.01
	92.60%	5.00%			
Awareness that PMKVY training is free	457	1	12.586	1	0.03
	99.80%	0.20%			

Figure 4.12 : Participation in Kaushal Melas and Awareness of PMKVY Training aspects

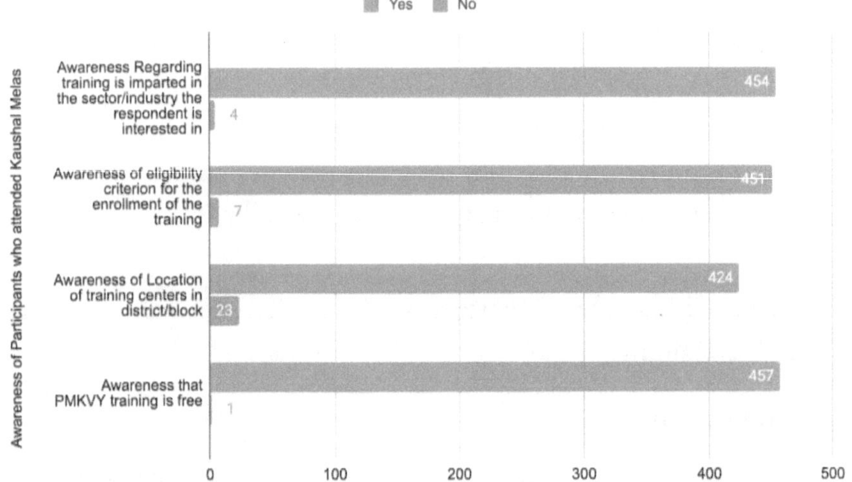

4.3.1.1 Awareness w.r.t. sector/industry of interest

We can reject the null hypothesis based on the Chi-square test results, indicating that there is a statistically significant positive relationship between these variables, $(1, 454) = 12.45$, p.05. As a result, there is a strong link between youth involvement in the Kaushal Melas and their awareness of the sector/industry in which training will be provided. The cross-tabulations also revealed that the vast majority of respondents (99.1%) who took part in Kaushal Melas learned about training opportunities in the sector/industry of their choice.

4.3.1.2 Awareness of eligibility criterion for the enrollment of the training

The Chi-square test results indicate that there is a positive relationship between participation in Kaushal Melas and awareness of the eligibility condition for enrolment in the programme, (1, N = 451) = 18.197, p.05. The cross-tabulations revealed that the majority of Kaushal Melas participants (98.5 percent) were aware of the eligibility conditions for enrolling in the programme.

4.3.1.3 Awareness of Location of training centers in district/block

The Chi-square test verified the positive relationship between Kaushal Melas participation and awareness of training centre locations in district/block, (1, N = 424) = 13.269, p.05. The cross-tabulations revealed that the majority of Kaushal Melas participants (92.6 percent) were aware of the locations of training facilities in districts/blocks.

4.3.1.4 Awareness that PMKVY training is free

The Chi-square test results indicate that there is a positive relationship between involvement in Kaushal Melas and awareness of the free PMKVY training (1, N = 457) = 12.586, p.001. According to the cross-tabulations, the vast majority of respondents (99.8%) who took part in Kaushal Melas learned that PMKVY training is free.

4.4 Beneficiary's Participation Kaushal Melas

Table 4.13: Beneficiary's Participation Kaushal Melas

Beneficiary's Participation Kaushal Melas		
	Frequency	**Percent**
Yes	458	56.1
No	358	43.9
Total	**816**	**100**

Figure 4.13: Beneficiary's Participation Kaushal Melas

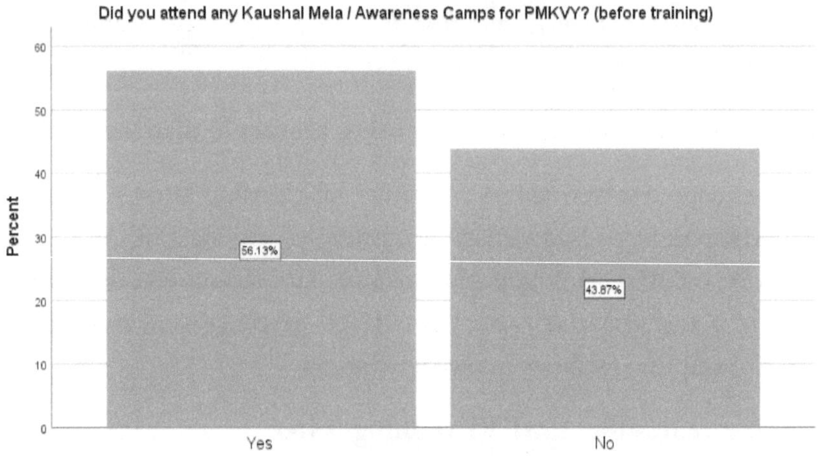

4.5 Beneficiary's Aspirations for the training sector and Training imparted under PMKVY

It might be assumed that the maximum of the respondents was mainly interested in receiving training in sectors such as Tourism & Hospitality (10.3%), automobiles (11.8%), beauty and wellness (19%) and retail (6.5%). The respondents were also interested in Agriculture and Apparel training.

Table 4.14: Training Sector of Interest and Training Imparted

Training Sectors	Training Sector of Interest Frequency	Training Sector of Interest Percent %	Training Imparted in Sector Frequency	Training Imparted in Sector Percent %
BFSI (Accounts)	19	2.3	17	2.1
Agriculture	51	6.3	110	13.5
Apparel	55	6.7	56	6.9
Automotive	96	11.8	99	12.1
BFSI	1	0.1	1	0.1
Beauty & Wellness	155	19	150	18.4

Training Sectors	Training Sector of Interest Frequency	Training Sector of Interest Percent %	Training Imparted in Sector Frequency	Training Imparted in Sector Percent %
IT-ITES (Call Centre)	34	4.2	31	3.8
Construction	8	1	6	0.7
Construction (Electrical)	33	4	33	4
Electronics	44	5.4	42	5.1
Apparel (Fashion)	5	0.6	3	0.4
Tourism and Hospitality (Food & Beverage)	7	0.9	7	0.9
IT-ITES (Hardware)	1	0.1	1	0.1
Tourism & Hospitality	84	10.3	103	12.6
IT-ITES	13	1.6	9	1.1
Automotive (Mechanical)	2	0.2	1	0.1
Healthcare (Nursing)	20	2.5	17	2.1
Retail	53	6.5	54	6.6
Management & Entrepreneurship (Soft Skills)	0	0	1	0.1
Management & Entrepreneurship (Trainer)	3	0.4	2	0.2
Telecom	22	2.7	23	2.8
Any other Sector	110	13.5	50	6.4
Total	**816**	**100**	**816**	**100**

It can be inferred from the analysis that majority of the respondents were able to undertake training in the sectors as, beauty and wellness (18.4%) Tourism & Hospitality (12.6%), Automobiles (12.1%), Agriculture (13.5%), retail (6.6%) So, there is a congruity in their training sectors of interest and the trainings undertaken by them in those sectors.

Figure 4.14: Training Preferences and Training Undergone

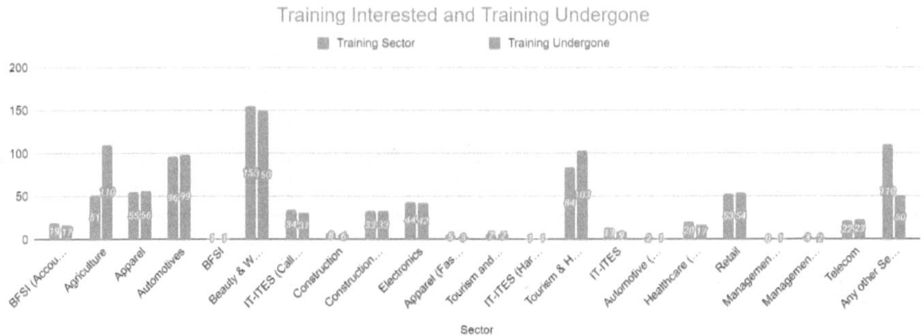

Table 4.15: Number of Respondents who got training in the Preferred Sector

Got Training Sector Interested in		
	Frequency	**Percent**
Yes	794	97.3
No	22	2.7
Total	**816**	**100**

It can be inferred from the table and figure that most of the sectors were congruous in terms of the respondent's aspiration and the imparted training to them.

Figure 4.15: Number of Respondents who got training in the Preferred Sector

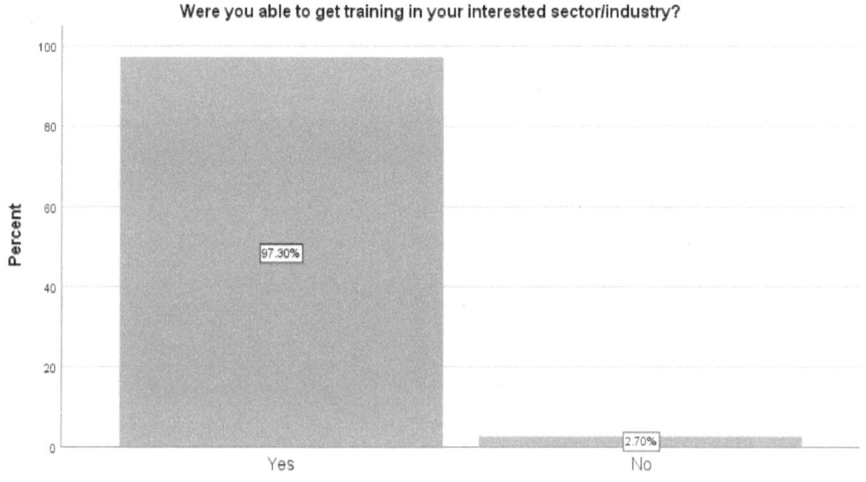

Processional Delivery

4.6 Delivery Mechanisms of PMKVY Trainings

4.6.1 Accessibility of the Training Centres

Table 4.16: Training Centres' Accessibility

Accessibility		
	Frequency	**Percent**
Yes	781	95.7
No	35	4.3
Total	**816**	**100**

Figure 4.16: Training Centres' Accessibility

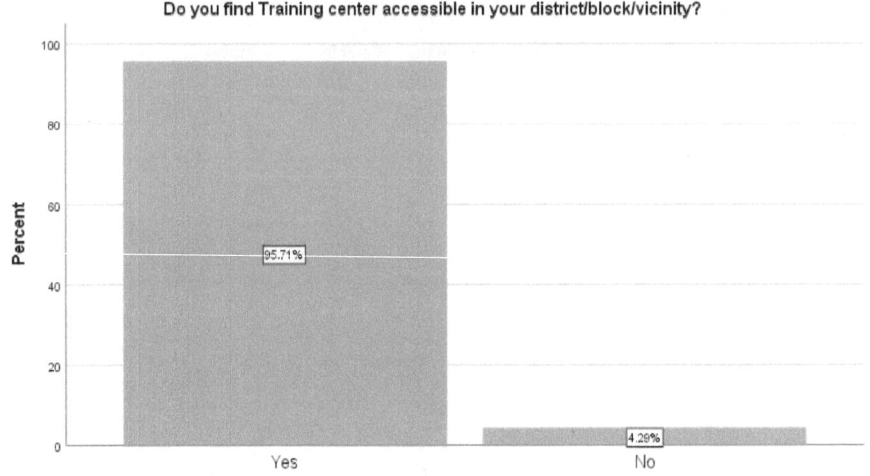

It can be inferred that training centres are accessible to more than 95% of the beneficiaries.

4.6.2 Provision of the Training in the Preferred Sector at the Centre

Table 4.17: Provision of the Training in the Preferred Sector

Provision of the Training in the Preferred Sector		
	Frequency	**Percent**
Yes	790	96.8
No	26	3.2
Total	**816**	**100**

The analysis has revealed that the preferred training sector is available to more than 96 % of the beneficiaries

Figure 4.17: Provision of the Training in the Preferred Sector

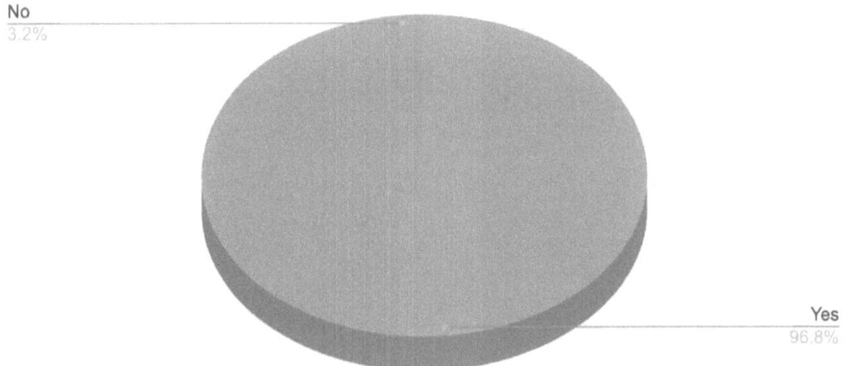

4.6.3 Ease in Enrolment at the Training Centre

Table 4.18: Enrolment at the Training Centre

Ease in the Enrolment		
	Frequency	**Percent**
Yes	798	97.8
No	18	2.2
Total	**816**	**100**

Figure 4.18: Ease in Enrolment at the Training Centre

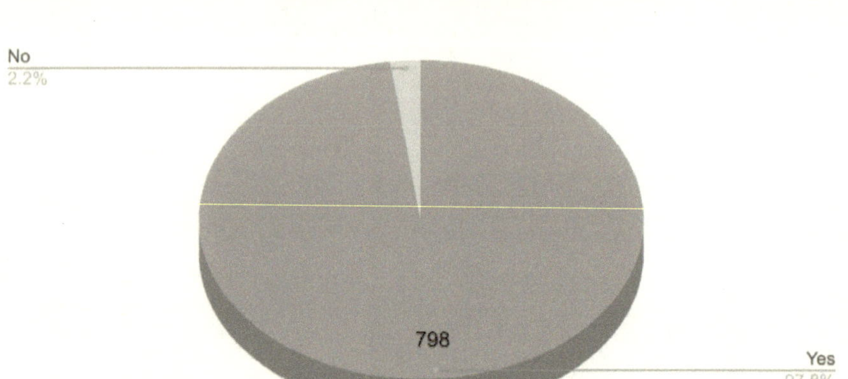

It can be inferred that the enrolment is easy for the PMKVY training as pointed out by 97.8% of the beneficiaries.

4.6.4 Duration of the PMKVY Training

Table 4.19: Duration of the Training

Duration		
	Frequency	**Percent**
3 months	465	57
4 months	278	34.1
5 months	51	6.3
6 months	17	2.1
More than 6 months	5	0.6
Total	**816**	**100**

Figure 4.19: Duration of the Training

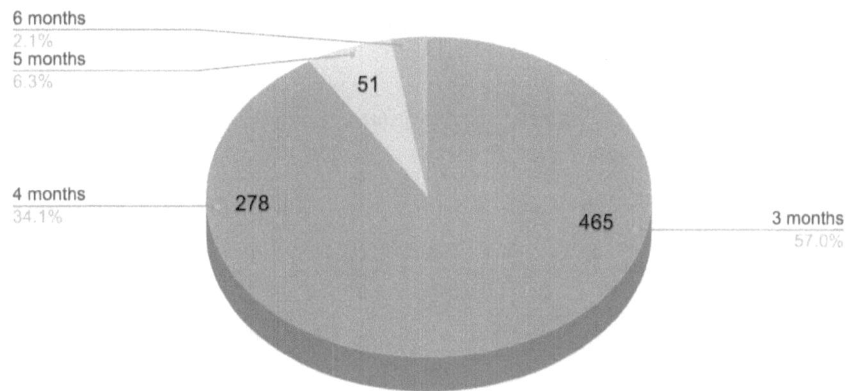

Most of the training was of 3 months (57%) followed by 4 months (34.1%). Only less than 10% of the training was of longer duration.

4.6.4 Method of Conduct of the PMKVY Training Sessions

Table 4.20: Conduct of the Training Sessions

Conduct of the Training Sessions		
	Frequency	**Percent**
Classroom	86	10.5
Practical	23	2.8
Both	707	86.6
Total	816	100

Figure 4.20: Conduct of the Training Sessions

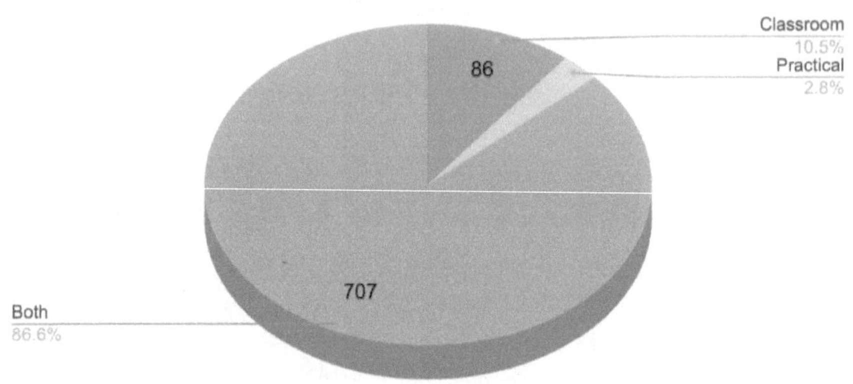

It can be inferred that both classroom and practical training sessions were being conducted under PMKVY.

Outcome of the Study

4.7 Components of PMKVY Trainings

4.7.1 Exploratory factor Analysis

In order to aggregate distinct factor components of the PMKVY training, the Exploratory factor Analysis (using Principal Component Analysis technique) was used to extract the various components of the PMKVY training. The KMO and Bartlett's Test of Sphericity were used to determine the suitability of conducting EFA in the first place. The findings confirm data adequacy for EFA, as Bartlett's test of sphericity (2 (153) = 18386.523, Vp.05 was significant, as was the big value of "Kaiser-Meyer-Olkin (KMO) Measure of Sampling Adequacy," which was 0.954. To extract the factors, eigen value criteria with 'varimax' rotation were used (Hair et al., 1984).

Table 4.21: KMO and Bartlett's Test

KMO and Bartlett's Test		
Kaiser-Meyer-Olkin Measure of Sampling Adequacy.		0.954
Bartlett's Test of Sphericity	Approx. Chi-Square	18386.523
	Df	153
	Sig.	0

Figure 4.21: Scree Plot

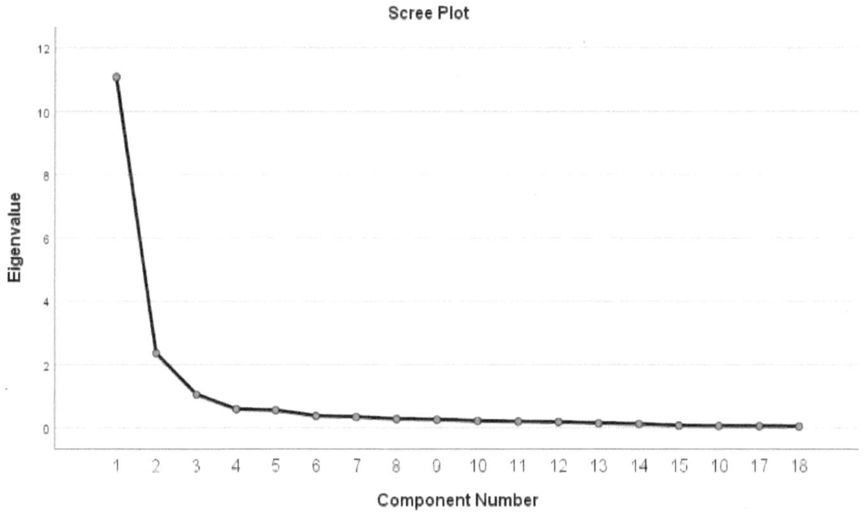

Table 4.22: Factor Loadings, Variance and Reliability

Factor	Statement	Item Code	Factor Loading	Variance (%)	Reliability Cronbach Alpha
Training Quality	Efficiency of the trainer	Trg2	0.905	27.757	0.986
	Instructors were professionals and trained in their expertise	Trg3	0.888		
	Outside Experts	Trg4	0.861		
	Trainers' friendliness	Trg5	0.896		
	Clarity in Instructions	Trg6	0.881		
Resources and Support	Quality of Training Material Provided to the Candidates	Trg7	0.74	19.872	0.921
	Resource material was relevant	Trg8	0.779		
	Depth and coverage of the resource material	Trg9	0.794		

Factor	Statement	Item Code	Factor Loading	Variance (%)	Reliability Cronbach Alpha
	Quality of the training	Trg1	0.724		
	Counseling Support	Trg10	0.568		
Infrastructure	Counseling facility	Inf1	0.781	32.964	0.948
	Tools	Inf2	0.81		
	Certified trainers	Inf3	0.822		
	Lab	Inf4	0.821		
	Toilets	Inf5	0.779		
	No. of classrooms	Inf6	0.781		
	Computers Facility	Inf7	0.767		
	Practice Area	Inf8	0.783		

The results of the Exploratory Factor Analysis suggest that three primary factors (with Eigenvalues >1) may be recovered as the principal component factors of the PMKVY training: Infrastructure Facilities, Training Quality, and Resources and Support.

Table 4.23: Means Values of Beneficiary's Perception

Means Values of Beneficiary's Perception on Training Parameters				
Training Parameters	Sub Items	Item Code	Mean	Std. Deviation
Training Quality	Efficiency of the trainer	Trg2	3.66	1.44
	Instructors were professionals and trained in their expertise	Trg3	3.52	1.366
	Outside Experts	Trg4	3.48	1.357
	Trainers' friendliness	Trg5	3.51	1.382
	Clarity in Instructions	Trg6	3.5	1.386
Resources and Support	Quality of Training Material Provided to the Candidates	Trg7	3.99	1.105
	Resource material was relevant	Trg8	3.83	1.193
	Depth and coverage of the resource material	Trg9	3.83	1.203
	Quality of the training	Trg1	3.89	1.211
	Counseling Support	Trg10	4.02	1.06
Infrastructure Facilities	Counseling facility	Inf1	4.17	0.899
	Tools	Inf2	4.16	0.859
	Certified trainers	Inf3	4.19	0.894
	Lab	Inf4	4.12	0.882
	Toilets	Inf5	4.03	0.932
	No. of classrooms	Inf6	4.07	0.925
	Computers Facility	Inf7	4.06	0.883
	Practice Area	Inf8	4.1	0.857

4.7.2 Confirmatory Factor Analysis

CFA is recommended and used to confirm construct validity, laying the groundwork for investigating the link between constructs and their components. Figure 4.23 depicts major model constructions based on the nature of latent variables or constructs. According to Holtzman and Leich (2014), there are a number of fit statistics that may be used to assess the model's fitness for the data in Table 4.24.

The model is fitted to the data in Table 4.24, as CFI is greater than 0.90, which is regarded acceptable. The SRMR value is less than 0.069, which is better than 0.08.

Table 4.24: Model Fit Measures

Model	NFI Delta1	RFI rho1	IFI Delta2	TLI rho2	CFI
Default model	0.94	0.93	0.95	0.94	0.95
Saturated model	1		1		1
Independence model	0	0	0	0	0

Validity Assessment

Table 4.25: Convergent and Discriminant Validity

Validity Measures			
	CR	AVE	MSV
IF	0.948	0.697	0.526
TQ	0.986	0.936	0.532
RS	0.923	0.708	0.532

CR > 0.7; AVE CR; 0.5 AVE) Convergent validity assessment Discriminant Validity: (AVE > MSV, ASVAVE) For all parameters, the CR is greater than 0.7 and the AVE is greater than 0.5, as shown in Table 4.25. In addition, the table indicates that CR outperforms AVE across the board. As a result, we can conclude that the measurement model's elements have appropriate convergent validity. MSV is less than AVE for all parameters, according to the measuring model. In addition, for all of the components, ASV is less than AVE. As a result, we can confirm the measurement model's discriminant validity.

Table 4.25 illustrates that the elements of the measurement model have convergent and discriminant validity, since the values of all constructs are acceptable. The model was found to be a good fit in the current situation.

Figure 4.22: CFA Model

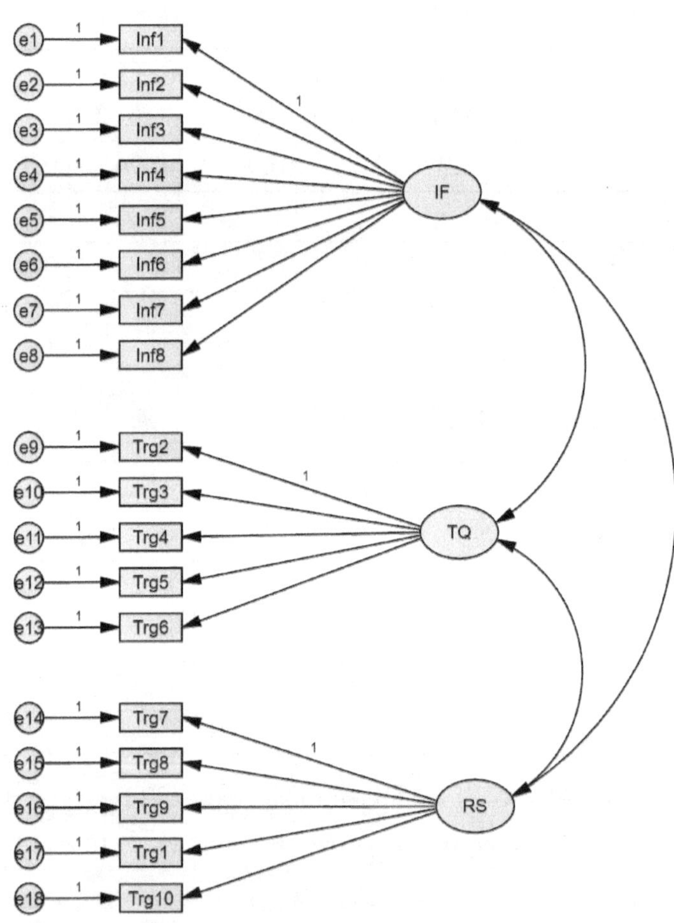

Table 4.26: Unstandardised and Standardised Regression Weights

			Unstandardised Regression Weights				Standardized Regression Weights
			Estimate	S.E.	C.R.	P	Estimate
Inf1	←	IF	1				0.84
Inf2	←	IF	0.99	0.03	31.72	***	0.87
Inf3	←	IF	1.03	0.03	31.79	***	0.87
Inf4	←	IF	1.01	0.03	31.59	***	0.86
Inf5	←	IF	1.05	0.03	30.84	***	0.85
Inf6	←	IF	1.01	0.03	29.26	***	0.82
Inf7	←	IF	0.91	0.03	26.79	***	0.78
Inf8	←	IF	0.89	0.03	27	***	0.78
Trg2	←	TQ	1				0.97
Trg3	←	TQ	0.95	0.01	79.92	***	0.97
Trg4	←	TQ	0.94	0.01	75.05	***	0.96
Trg5	←	TQ	0.96	0.01	77.53	***	0.97
Trg6	←	TQ	0.96	0.01	76.04	***	0.96
Trg7	←	RS	1				0.91
Trg8	←	RS	1.09	0.03	42.22	***	0.92
Trg9	←	RS	1.1	0.03	41.68	***	0.91
Trg1	←	RS	0.94	0.03	29.68	***	0.78
Trg10	←	RS	0.7	0.03	22.69	***	0.66

*** Significant at p<0.05

Finally, the EFA and CFA findings revealed that the three key component aspects of the PMKVY training were Training Quality, Resources and Support, and Infrastructure Facilities.

In addition to this, the trainees' perceptions effectiveness of the PMKVY trainings (in terms of skill enhancement, satisfaction and standard of living) were also computed on their mean values for the Likert scaled data sets as mentioned below (Section 4.8)

4.8 Relationship between components of PMKVY Training and Effectiveness of PMKVY

Effectiveness is ascertained through i) skill enhancement of the trainees (employability skills, digital shills, soft skills) ii) Satisfaction of trainee youth beneficiaries, and iii) Standard of living

4.8.1 Relationship between components of PMKVY Training and Skills Enhancement of PMKVY

In the multiple regression analysis, the dependent variable skill enhancement of PMKVY was assessed to know the predictors (independent variables i.e., 3 components of PMKVY, Infrastructure, Training Quality, Resources and Support) impacting skill enhancement of the beneficiaries. The following are the results of the multiple regression analysis:

Table 4.27: Regression Coefficients - Standardised and Unstandardised with Significance Values on skill enhancement

Coefficients						
Model		Unstandardised Coefficients		Standardised Coefficients	t	
	R Square	B	Std. Error	Beta		Significance
(Constant)	0.172	4.155	0.026		162.576	0
Infrastructure		0.332	0.026	0.414	12.985	0
(Constant)	0.382	4.155	0.022		188.086	0
Infrastructure		0.332	0.022	0.414	15.023	0
Training Quality		0.368	0.022	0.459	16.628	0

Coefficients						
Model		**Unstandardised Coefficients**		**Standardised Coefficients**	**t**	
	R Square	**B**	**Std. Error**	**Beta**		**Significance**
Training Quality		0.368	0.017	0.459	21.053	0
Resources and Support		0.387	0.017	0.483	22.164	0

Regression Equation:

Skill enhancement = 0.332IF + 0.368 TQ + 0.387RS

Figure 4.23: Regression Model

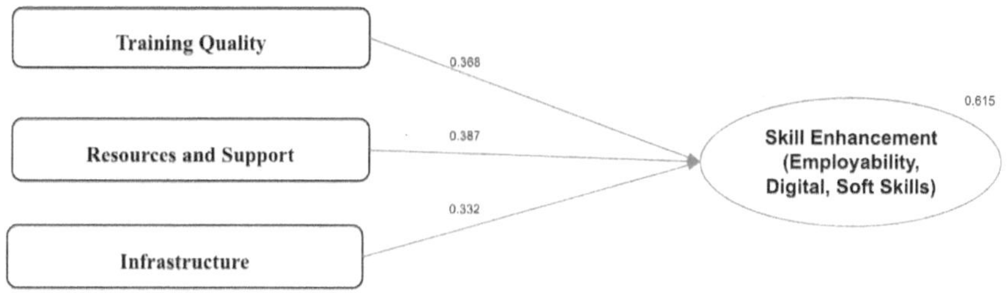

Interpretation

To further understand the relationship between determinants of PMKVY Training and skill enhancement in PMKVY, a stepwise regression analysis was used. In the first only infrastructure was taken into consideration and the standardised beta value is 0.414 at p<0.05. In the 2nd step Training Quality was found to be significant with a standardised beta value is 0.459 at p<0.05, though R sq was less.

In the third and final step, it can be interpreted from the regression analysis that there was a significant positive relationship of the skill enhancements with all the determinants of PMKVY trainings with standardised beta values Infrastructure 0.414, Training Quality - 0.459, Resources and Support - 0.483 with p values <0.05 (R sq 61.5%).

Thus, Resources and Support was the most important determinant followed by Training quality and then by Infrastructure.

4.8.2 Relationship between components of PMKVY Training and Satisfaction of Beneficiaries

In a similar vein, a multiple regression analysis was carried out with the dependent variable Satisfaction of PMKVY Beneficiaries and the predictors (independent variables i.e., three PMKVY components, Infrastructure, Training Quality, Resources, and Support) influencing Satisfaction of Beneficiaries. The following are the results of the multiple regression analysis:

Table 4.28: Regression Coefficients - Standardized and Unstandardised with Significance Values on Satisfaction

Coefficients						
Model		Unstandardized Coefficients		Standardized Coefficients		t	Sig.
	R Square	B	Std. Error	Beta		
(Constant)		4.214	0.024		172.698	0
Infrastructure	0.173	0.319	0.024	0.416	13.069	0
(Constant)		4.214	0.022		195.861	0
Infrastructure	0.358	0.319	0.022	0.416	14.822	0
Training Quality		0.329	0.022	0.43	15.297	0
(Constant)		4.214	0.017		242.357	0
Infrastructure	0.581	0.319	0.017	0.416	18.341	0
Training Quality		0.329	0.017	0.43	18.928	0
Resources and Support		0.362	0.017	0.472	20.804	0

Figure 4.24: Regression Model

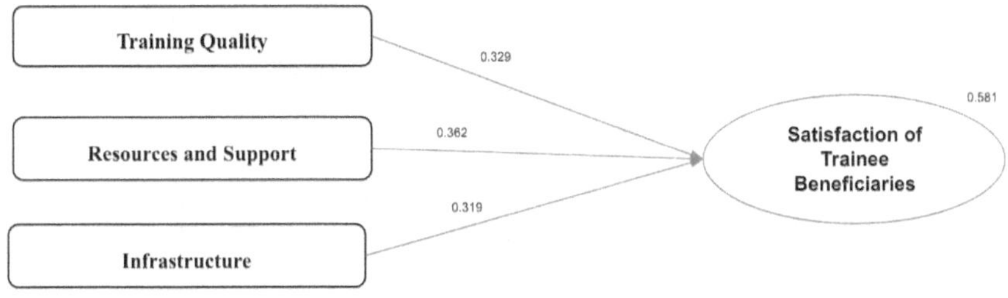

Interpretation

The link between factors of PMKVY Training and outcome/benefits as assessed by PMKVY participants in terms of Satisfaction was investigated using Stepwise Regression Analysis. Only infrastructure was included in the first, and the standardised beta value was 0.416 at p0.05. Training Quality was shown to be significant in the second phase, with a standardised beta value of 0.43 at p0.05, though R sq was lower.

The third and final phase revealed a significant positive connection between satisfaction and all factors of PMKVY training, with standardised beta values of Infrastructure 0.319, Training Quality 0.329, Resources and Support 0.362 and p values of 0.05. (R sq 61.5 percent).

Thus, Resources and Support was the most important determinant followed by training quality and then by infrastructure.

4.8.3 Relationship between components of PMKVY Training and Standard of Living of Beneficiaries

Finally, a multiple regression analysis was conducted with the dependent variable Standard of Living of PMKVY Beneficiaries and the predictors (independent variables i.e., three PMKVY components, Infrastructure, Training Quality, Resources, and Support) influencing Standard of Living of Beneficiaries. The following are the results of the multiple regression analysis:

Table 4.29: Regression Coefficients - Standardized and Unstandardised with Significance Values on Standard of Living of Beneficiaries

Coefficients						
Model		Unstandardized Coefficients		Standardized Coefficients	t	Sig.
	R Square	B	Std. Error	Beta		
(Constant)	0.155	4.08	0.033		125.44	0
Infrastructure		0.398	0.033	0.394	12.237	0
(Constant)	0.255	4.08	0.031		133.441	0
Infrastructure		0.398	0.031	0.394	13.018	0
Training Quality		0.318	0.031	0.315	10.4	0
(Constant)	0.462	4.08	0.026		157.02	0
Infrastructure		0.398	0.026	0.394	15.318	0
Training Quality		0.318	0.026	0.315	12.237	0
Resources and Support		0.46	0.026	0.456	17.712	0

Figure 4.25: Regression Model

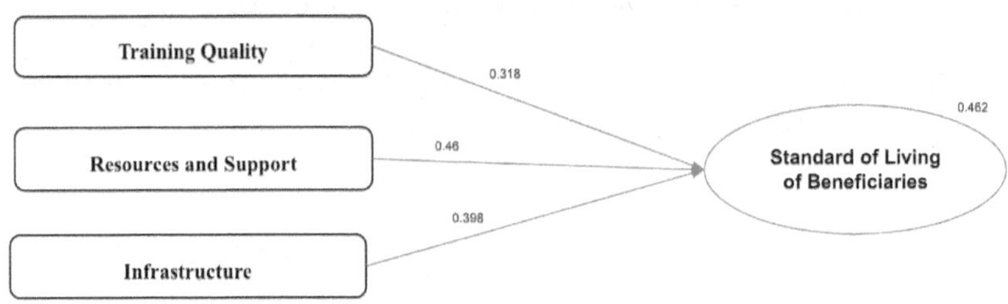

Stepwise Regression Analysis was performed to understand the relationship between determinants of PMKVY Training and outcome/benefits as perceived by the participants of PMKVY in terms of standard of living. In the first only infrastructure was taken into consideration and the standardised beta value is 0.394 at p<0.05. In the 2nd step Training Quality was found to be significant with a standardised beta value is 0.315 at p<0.05, though R sq was less.

In the third and final step, it can be interpreted that there was a significant positive relationship of the outcome/benefits - standard of living as perceived by the participants with all the determinants of PMKVY trainings with standardised beta values Infrastructure 0.398, Training Quality 0.318, Resources and Support 0.46 with p values <0.05 (R sq 61.5%).

Thus, Resources and Support was the most important determinant followed by Infrastructure and then by Training quality.

4.9 Conclusion

This chapter contains a detailed analysis of the study that reveals the tremendous impact of PMKVY training on Haryana's trainees and youth beneficiaries. The study's conclusions and recommendations are presented in the next chapter.

Chapter 5

Conclusions

5.1 Summary

This chapter summarizes the study's findings and recommendations regarding the effectiveness of PMKVY training in Haryana. It entails in-depth discussions with trainees/youth beneficiaries about their perceptions of various aspects and provisions of the PMKVY training, as well as determining their level of awareness, mobilization, and aspiration to pursue these training opportunities in a variety of sectors and job roles at affiliated training centers in their respective districts in Haryana. Thus, this chapter summarizes the study's findings and makes critical policy and operational suggestions in light of the study's findings, which extend beyond the boundaries of future research in this area.

5.2 Introduction

The major conclusions of this study are presented in each of the following subsections, as: -

5.2.1 Demographic profile

The main conclusions pertaining to the demographic profile of the 816 trainee youth beneficiaries in 13 selected districts of Haryana under the PMKVY training represents a viable composition of 387 male and 429 female trainees. Majority of them fell under three categories; a) youth in the age bracket of 18 to 24 years b) were unmarried and c) were belonging to a joint family with over 4 or 5family members. It can also be concluded that the majority of them were educated with senior secondary level qualification. Regarding the household income, it can be concluded that the respondents were moderate and this was also reflected in their low to average personal income. So, there is a lot of scope and potential in training and skilling the youths in Haryana for income generation and leading to sustainable livelihoods for them and their families.

5.2.2 Beneficiary's Participation in Kaushal Melas & Awareness on PMKVY Training

One of the basic PMKVY guidelines entail conduct of Kaushal Melas every six months for realizing the goal of widespread social and community mobilisation in the successful implementation of the PMKVY training. In accordance with this, PMKVY places a premium on involving target beneficiaries through a well-defined mobilization process. From the trainee/youth beneficiary perspective, the following significant findings and conclusions can be made:

To begin, the study findings indicate that trainees have a high level of awareness of PMKVY training aspects. The majority of youths were quite knowledgeable about PMKVY training and its various components, such as

- Training Sector of Interest
- eligibility criteria for the enrollment of PMKVY training
- availability of the training centers in the district
- provision of free-of-cost training

It can also be concluded in the study that there is ample evidence of satisfactory perception of PMKVY training, in terms of their accessibility, easy enrollment and training as per the trainees' aspirations. It was also observed that most of the training was of short duration of either 3 months or 4 months. There were relatively less training sessions which lasted more than 5 months. Most of the sessions were conducted both through classroom as well as practical. Thus, in this line of study, the summary table presents the conclusions generated from the results of Chi-Square tests used to analyze the relationship between trainees' participation in Kaushal Melas and their awareness of PMKVY training features (Table 5.1). There is a significant association between trainees' participation in the Kaushal Melas and their Awareness w.r.t. sector/industry of interest where training is imparted. The cross-tabulations revealed that the majority of the respondents who participated in Kaushal Melas were benefited and they became aware regarding training being imparted in the sector/industry of their interest.

There is a strong correlation between trainees' participation in Kaushal Melas and their level of awareness of the sector/industry in which training is delivered. The cross-tabulations demonstrated that the majority of respondents who participated in Kaushal Melas profited and gained knowledge about training available in their chosen sector/industry.

Similarly, it was deduced that there is a significant correlation between trainees' participation in Kaushal Melas and their awareness of the eligibility conditions for training enrollment. As a result of their participation in the Kaushal Melas, students gained a better understanding of the eligibility criteria for enrolment in the course.

Additionally, it can be established that there is a considerable relationship between trainees' participation in Kaushal Melas and their awareness of training facilities' locations in districts/blocks. As a result, the majority of youths were aware of the locations of training centers in their districts/blocks as a result of the Kaushal Melas.

Finally, it can be stated that there is a considerable correlation between trainees' participation in Kaushal Melas and their understanding of the free nature of PMKVY training. Attending Kaushal Melas benefited the trainees significantly, as they were motivated to pursue training in their areas of interest. Thus, the next step in the study was to compare the industries to which they aspired and the sectors in which they actually received training through the PMKVY.

Table 5.1: Summary of the Chi-square tests

Association between Beneficiary's Participation in Kaushal Melas and their Awareness PMKVY Trainings	
Hypotheses	**Result**
H1: There is no significant association between beneficiary's awareness on the Training Sector of Interest with their participation in Kaushal Mela under PMKVY.	Rejected
H2: There is no significant association between beneficiary's awareness on eligibility criteria for the enrollment in PMKVY training with their participation in Kaushal Mela under PMKVY.	Rejected
H3: There is no significant association between beneficiary's awareness on availability of the training centers in the district with their participation in Kaushal Mela under PMKVY.	Rejected
H4: There is no significant association between beneficiary's awareness that PMKVY training is free with their participation in Kaushal Mela under PMKVY.	Rejected

As a result, participation in the Kaushal Melas/awareness camps for this aim was also viewed positively by them. The findings indicate a positive correlation between beneficiary involvement in Kaushal Melas and awareness of PMKVY training.

5.2.3 Training sectors aspired & the training sectors undergone

The PMKVY training is successful only when the trainees are encouraged to come forward and undergo the training sessions in true spirit. This is possible only when there is a clear-cut match of the training imparted in the job roles/sectors as per the trainee's aspirations for those sectors. In this perspective, the following observations were derived: -

It can be concluded from the study findings that the most preferred **training sectors of interest** to the youth were in Beauty and Wellness, Automobiles Hospitality and Tourism, Apparels, Retail, Agriculture and Electronics.

Further, it can be concluded that most of the sectors **were congruous** in terms of the respondents' aspirations and the training was undergone by them in those sectors. However, **there is some gap in these two aspects in the case of** Agriculture, followed by Hospitality & Tourism. So, there is scope to further delve into and explore reasons for it.

5.2.4 Components of PMKVY Trainings

Next, the study unveiled the various components of PMKVY training elements. The results of the Exploratory Factor Analysis indicate that the primary determinants of PMKVY Training were as follows: -

Factor 1: Training Quality
Factor 2: Resources and Support.
Factor 3: Infrastructure

The Cronbach alpha (reliability) measures were also very good, (> 0.9) for each of these factors. It can be concluded that the main determinants of PMKVY Training in the order of variance was Infrastructure followed by Training Quality and finally Resources and Support.

These were also validated through the Confirmatory Factor Analysis results which prove the discriminant and convergent validity of the factor constructs and their items.

Table 5.2: PMKVY Training Components

PMKVY Training Components	
Training Components	**Sub-components**
Training Quality	Efficiency of the trainer
	Instructors were professionals and trained in their expertise
	Outside Experts
	Trainers' friendliness
	Clarity in Instructions

PMKVY Training Components	
Training Components	**Sub-components**
Resources and Support	Quality of Training Material Provided to the Candidates
	Resource material was relevant
	Depth and coverage of the resource material
	Quality of the training
	Counseling Support
Infrastructure Facilities	Counseling facility
	Tools
	Certified trainers
	Lab
	Toilets
	No. of classrooms
	Computers Facility
	Practice Area

5.2.5 Relationship between components of PMKVY Training and Effectiveness of PMKVY

The study, the effectiveness of PMKVY is ascertained through the perceived benefits accruing to the trainee/youth beneficiaries in terms of these 3 aspects, as- i)Skill enhancement of the trainees (i.e. digital skills, soft skills and employability skills), and ii) Satisfaction of trainee/youth beneficiaries, and iii) improvement in their Standard of living. This was examined through Multiple Regression analysis, the conclusions for which are given below:-

Table 5.3: Summary of Regression results

Relationship between components of PMKVY Trainings and Effectiveness of PMKVY	
H5: There is no significant relationship between Training Quality and skill enhancement of PMKVY	Rejected
H6: There is no significant relationship between Resources and Support and skill enhancement of PMKVY	Rejected
H7: There is no significant relationship between Infrastructure and skill enhancement of PMKVY	Rejected
H8: There is no significant relationship between Training Quality and Satisfaction of Beneficiaries	Rejected
H9: There is no significant relationship between Resources & Support and Satisfaction of Beneficiaries	Rejected
H10: There is v significant relationship between Infrastructure and Satisfaction of Beneficiaries	Rejected
H11: There is no significant relationship between Training Quality and Standard of Living of Beneficiaries	Rejected
H12: There is no significant relationship between Resources and Support and Standard of Living of Beneficiaries	Rejected
H13: There is no significant relationship between Infrastructure and Standard of Living of Beneficiaries	Rejected

According to the regression analysis, there was a substantial positive link between **skill enhancement** and all of the components of PMKVY training. The most important determinant was **resources and support**, followed by training quality and infrastructure.

Additionally, a significant positive association between satisfaction and all components of PMKVY training may be determined. Additionally, it can be stated that there was a statistically significant positive link between the outcome benefits - **standard of living** and all of the PMKVY training components. The most critical determinant was **resources and support,** followed by infrastructure and finally training quality. Thus, in each of these circumstances, the most critical component of increasing the effectiveness of the PMKVY training was resources and support.

To summarize, as indicated previously in the conclusions, the majority of trainees got pre-enrolment counselling and were encouraged to attend periodic Kaushal Melas. Additionally, they received training materials. However, placement assistance should be expanded. In general, beneficiaries had a favourable impression of the PMKVY training components on most dimensions, particularly trainer quality, content and curriculum adequacy, and training quality. The following section summarizes the study's principal recommendations.

5.3 Recommendations

This section presents key policy and operational recommendations based on the evaluation of PMKVY training from trainee/youth beneficiary's perspective along with the inputs provided by the Training partners, trainees at the training centres where they were enrolled and undergoing the training. These are presented in this section.

5.3.1 Policy Recommendations

It can be recommended that a major prerogative in the PMKVY should be skilling should be demand driven while ensuring minimum migration. For this, the skill gap assessment is of paramount importance. Social mobilization, sensitizing the youth to get skilled to fill skill gaps, selecting the sector as per the youth's aspirations are important aspects for the skilling under PMKVY.

The skilling should be specifically aligned as per the industry requirements. Up skilling the existing workforce should be a continuous process to remain relevant and productive. Duration of skilling should be made medium to short, including bridge courses to cover competency gaps.

The awareness of the PMKVY scheme to the target population, its salient aspects and benefits, skill centres available, the fact that skilling is free of cost, counseling centres to guide selection of the sectors and job roles to meet the trainees aspirations, linkages with the industry for the jobs are some of the important aspects for the successful implementation of the PMKVY. In this regard, different sources of information, involving the electronic, social and print media, advertising and mobile applications, campaigns at the schools, road shows, Kaushal Melas, Centralized call centres to answer queries, involvement of the self-help groups for social mobilization are some of the influential sources for creating awareness and informing the youth and experienced workforce . More importantly, the existing trainees can be utilized to encourage potential youths to be a part of the PMKVY training. They will constitute as main reference groups in influencing the non-trainees in other regions as well. The experienced youths can be tapped and further trained in the role of trainers.

To guarantee the PMKVY is delivered effectively, it is critical to establish a comprehensive monitoring and evaluation structure to verify that the skill is imparted by training partners in accordance with established standards and that the training is of a high quality.

Accessibility of the skill centres to the youth through geographical spread, selection of job roles as per the skill gap, creating adequate certified trainers, ensuring high quality infrastructure and delivery mechanism, availability of the handbooks and other training material and skilling as per the National Skill Qualification Framework aligned courses, allocating targets as per the demand, industry participation in skilling are of paramount importance to strengthen the skill ecosystem. The provision of skill certification and reward will attract more candidates and enable them to get employment in different job roles in the industry.

Industry participation is skilling, preference to employ skilled and certified trainees, skill premium; paid model (partial payment of fees) of skilling for high demand jobs will help in financial sustainability and scalability of the scheme. Paid model helps in ensuring that the training program is taken more seriously by the trainees and skill infrastructure improved.

As the pace of the program has substantially increased with time, the institutional capacity building at the district level in the form of District Skill Committee(s) to implement the scheme, advocacy, monitoring and evaluation, skill gap identification to meet local demand, linkages with the industry to meet their demand, organise Kaushal Melas and job camps will enhance the scale, speed and high standards of the scheme. Recognition of vocational education through various social events as a value-add and improving employability of the youth will make it more aspirational.

5.3.2 Operational Recommendations

Any training program's effectiveness is contingent upon a proper fit between the training objective and the prospective learners' objective and interest in receiving the training in true spirits. Thus, it is essential that proper pre-screening of candidates be conducted prior to enrolling them in the training program. Prior to enrolling in the training program, it must be verified that prospective trainees grasp the job needs and expectations.

Following that, it might be recommended that youth be adequately mobilized to engage in serious training at associated training centers in their district. To organize teenagers, numerous sources of information can be utilized, including television/radio commercials, door-to-door campaigning and board/hoardings, social media, and even local meetings and gatherings.

According to the trainees' perspectives, they required increased connection with industry experts and also placement support in order to obtain employment in the job roles for which they obtained training. This is critical for policymakers to ensure that trainees obtain jobs in the training sectors to which they aim and in the job roles to which they aspire. As a result, it is advised that the program's placement aid be strengthened. Additionally, a strong emphasis should be placed on counseling, mentoring, and assistance and support provided to trainees.

Innovative ways for monitoring program implementation must be identified. Training providers have said that given the present documentation requirements, it is impossible for them to demonstrate the self-employment of a large number of qualified candidates. As a result, novel solutions to this challenge must be identified.

Additionally, it can be advised that a provision for 'trainer development and certification' be included with the goal of developing a pool of high-quality trainers/instructors capable of imparting instruction under PMKVY. They should receive specific incentives to reward their efforts in this area of skilling and upskilling rural youth, particularly those who may have a disability or are marginalized members of society.

Additionally, the PMKVY training course curriculum should be matched with industry requirements in order to boost youth employability and capabilities. Regular and timely assessment and feedback systems might be critical in developing the youth's abilities and competence. To ensure successful performance on assessment exams, protocols must be developed to ensure that trainees are evaluated on a regular basis during their training. Collaboration with industry specialists and academia may be arranged to maximize the impact of PMKVY training in a particular location.

Infrastructure facilities should be handled appropriately and their upkeep and repair performed on a timely basis. To the benefit of trainees, resource materials should be supplied to guarantee that training manuals are available in regional languages. The innovative training centers' achievements should be recognized and rewarded appropriately.

5.4 Limitations of Study

Like any research study, there are some constraints that delimit the scope of the study but nominally. The main constraints were on account of paucity of time and coverage apart from response generation from the trainee participants. Besides, the study encountered some response biases and prevalence of situational and subjective intervening variables which was uncontrollable given the nature of the study. Even some sampling error might have crept in this study. "Sampling errors arise from estimating a population characteristic by looking at only one portion of the population rather than the entire population," Cooper and Schindler, (2006), as the sample was confined only to the PMKVY trainees in Haryana, so this limited the study. A further generalization of this study for other geographical locations where PMKVY is implemented has to be used with caution as cultural and socio-economic backgrounds may differ. So, generalization was difficult as the sampling frame was restricted only to the PMKVY trainees in Haryana. Any further adaptations to the other locations have to be realized with caution. Another limitation was of eliciting accurate responses from the inexperienced youth who were not too eager to participate in the survey initially. So, they had to be counseled and, in this exercise, the help of Training partners was also taken while getting the questionnaires filled at the centre. However, through reliability and validity tests efforts to minimize response error have been attempted and a large representative sample size was drawn to overcome the response biases and improve the errors. Nevertheless, scope as well as significance of this study far outweighs these limitations that were encountered in the study.

5.5 Scope of Study

This study provided rich insights to understand the trainees' perceptions about the PMKVY 2.0 spread across 13 districts in Haryana. Each and every aspect of the PMKVY right from the awareness to mobilization, aspiration, conduct and the components of the PMKVY training have been elucidated from the youth's perspective. In addition, the study extends to relate these perceptual components of PMKVY with the effectiveness of PMKVY in terms of outcome benefits accruing to the youths (as Skill enhancement, Satisfaction, and Standard of living).

In light of this, major policy recommendations and operational recommendations were highlighted, as mentioned above, and this paves the way forward for the effective implementation of the PMKVY.

So, the scope of this study extends to similar studies in other locations where PMKVY is implemented and with the rolling out of the PMKVY 3.0 in

January 2021, this becomes even more important. The study is quantitative in nature but given the subjective elements involved, it can be stated that both quantitative and qualitative study approach, using the triangulation method involving several key stakeholders involved in the PMKVY implementation would lend a wide scope to the subject matter. So, the scope of the study extends to studies using both quantitative and qualitative analysis involving other stakeholders, such as Training partners and allied institutions and experts of the PMKVY.

Further, in the study only the trainee participants were considered. So, a comparative study between participants and non-participants as comparison groups can also widen the scope of the study. Taking the views of the non-participants of PMKVY will elicit reasons why they are reluctant to undergo training and in turn, point to the effectiveness of the PMKVY training.

Another scope of the study can be evinced by conducting comparative analysis during training and post-training responses to ascertain whether the trainees actually got employed or started their own ventures. Moreover, a longitudinal study in this context will further extend the scope and other studies can be conducted on these lines.

Finally, but certainly not least, the study's scope underlines the possibility of studies focused to the PMKVY's Recognition of Prior Learning (RPL) All this will lead to immense contribution in drawing a framework for effective implementation of various training programs and provisions in the skilling ecosystems.

Epilogue

A book is a bundle of thoughts, experiences, inner engineering and even the idiosyncrasies of the authors. Since the research and the related studies came to an end by 2021 OR at the most by early 2022, so to say; it is the onerous responsibility of the authors to make it temporal; updated and latest. Therefore, this part of the book is needed and that too in the macro context of PMKVY.

India is the 'most populated country' in the world apropos the enormous number of unemployed youth. On the one hand, the skilled manpower is not available in the talent market; and, on the other hand; the young people are sitting idle without any work and are simply killing the time. With a view to this conundrum, PMKVY becomes the panacea for gainful purposes of meeting the requirements of industries and unemployed young people both alike. Cumulatively PMKVY (1.0, 2.0. 3.0) have trained 1,37,24,226, assessed 1,24,54,593 and certified 1,10,34 285 candidates as per the PMKVY Dash Board as on 09 July 2023. Orders regarding Constitution of Steering Committee for PMKVY 4.0 and Executive Committee for Skill Hub for implementation of PMKVY 4.0 have been issued. However, approval of the PMKVY 4.0 by the cabinet is awaited.

The prognosis of PMKVY perse, lies in its implementation; other factors enumerated interalia, in this book.

References

1. Aaker, D. A., Kumar, V., & Day, G. S. (2008), Marketing Research. John Wiley & Sons.

2. Abhishek, V., & Aditya, S. (2015). Skill Development Programmes: A Project Management Perspective. *International Journal of Humanities and Management Sciences (IJHMS)*, *3*(05). 358-364

3. Adams, A. V. (2007), The role of youth skills development in the transition to work: A global review. Children & Youth, World Bank.

4. Agrawal, M., & Thakur, K. S. (2019), Impact of Pradhan Mantri Kaushal Vikas Yojana on the Productivity of Youth in Gwalior Region, India. *International Journal of Recent Technology and Engineering (IJRTE)*, 8 (4), 801-806

5. Agrawal, T., & Agrawal, A. (2017), Vocational education and training in India: a labour market perspective. *Journal of Vocational Education & Training*, *69*(2), 246-265.

6. Agrawal, T. (2014), Skill development in India: an examination. *Journal of Education and Work*, *27*(6), 629-650.

7. Amandeep &Brar K. K (2015), Skill Development in Higher Education: Trends and Issue. *International Journal of Emerging Research in Management &Technology*, 4(2), 126-130.

8. Ansari, Hamid (2015), Skill Development, Critical for faster economic growth, https://m.economictimes.com/news/economy/policy/skill-development-critical-for-faster-economic-growth-hamid-ansari/articleshow/46964343.cms

9. Ansari, T. H. and Khan, M. A, (2018), Role of Education and Skill Development to Promote Employment in India, Available

online at: https://www.researchgate.net/publication/329782820 TY - CHAP

10. Bhiwa, G. S. (2014), Skill Development – An Engine of Economic Growth. *Tactful Management Research Journal, 89-92*

11. Bhuvana S., Kavya and Geetanjali P. (2019) A Study on Effectiveness of Pradhan Mantri Kaushal Vikas Yojana Centres in Bengaluru Regions *UAS - JMC*, 4 (2). 22-25

12. Boyd, H.W., Westfall, R. and Stasch, F.S. (1999). Marketing Research – Text and Cases. Richard D. Irwin, Inc.

13. Brown, B, L (2001). Does Training Generally Work? The Returns to In-Company Training. *Industrial and Labour Relations Review* 54 (3), 647-662.

14. Bryman, A., and Bell, E. (2015). Business Research Methods (4th Ed.). Oxford: Oxford University Press

15. Bureau, L. (2004). Indian Labour Year Book. *New Delhi: Ministry of Labour and Employment, Government of India.*

16. Business Standard (2017), Why India's skill mission has failed, https://www.business-standard.com/article/economy-policy/why-india-s-skill-mission-has-failed-117090200098_1.html

17. Cabral, C. &Dhar, R. L. (2019). Skill development research in India: a systematic literature review and future research agenda. *Benchmarking: An International Journal.*

18. Central Statistical Organization, India. (2007). National Accounts Statistics: sources and Methods

19. Chand, R., Srivastava, S. K., & Singh, J. (2017). Changes in the rural economy of India, 1971 to 2012. *Economic & Political Weekly, 52*(52), 65.

20. Chandrasekaran N, Anbuthambi B. (2017), Impact of Skill India on Rural Youth – A Perspective, *ICTACT Journal on Management Studies*, 3(1), 457-460.

21. Chavda, M. D., & Trivedi, B. S. (2015). Impact of Age on Skills Development in Different Groups of Students. *International Journal of Information and Education Technology*, 5(1), 55-59. doi:10.7763/ijiet. 2015.v5.476

22. Chenoy, D., Ghosh, S. M., & Shukla, S. K. (2019). Skill development for accelerating the manufacturing sector: the role of 'new-age' skills for 'Make in India'. *International Journal of Training Research*, *17*(sup1), 112-130.

23. Chenoy, D. (2016). Skill development in India: A transformation in the making. In *India Infrastructure Report 2012*, 237-245, Routledge India.

24. Chenoy D. (2012). Skill Development in India: A Transformation in the Making. India Infrastructure Report

25. Churchill, G. A., Brown, T. J., & Suter, T. A. (1996). *Basic Marketing Research*. Orlando, FL: Dryden Press.

26. Cochran W.G. (1980) Fisher and the Analysis of Variance. In: Fienberg S.E., Hinkley D.V. (eds) R.A. Fisher: An Appreciation. Lecture Notes in Statistics, vol 1. *Springer*, New York, NY. https://doi.org/10.1007/978-1-4612-6079-0_4

27. Cooper, D., and Schindler, P. (2006). Business research methods (9th Illustrated edition). New York, McGraw-Hill/Irwin.

28. Dash, C. S., & Dash (2020), S. Skill Development Mission and the Skill Landscape of India-An Empirical Study https://ijisrt.com/assets/upload/files/IJISRT20OCT335.pdf

29. Deka, R. J &Batra, B. (2016). The Scope of Skill Development, Employability of Indian Workforce in Context of Make in India: A Study. *International Journal of Engineering Technology, Management and Applied Sciences*, 4(4), 68-75

30. Denscombe, M. (2009), Item non-response rates: a comparison of online and paper questionnaires, *International Journal of Social Research Methodology*, 12(4), 281–91

31. Different bodies of skilling India http://ficci.in/spdocument/20405/FICCI-KPMG-Global-Skills-report.pdf

32. Divyaranjani, R. &Rajasekar, D. (2017). A research on effectiveness of Training and development on Worker's productivity in automobile Manufacturing companies with Reference to Chennai city. *International Journal of Civil Engineering and Technology*, 8(6), 19–30.

33. E&Y (2018), Where are we on skills, https://www.ey.com/in/en/industries/india-sectors/education/knowledge-paper-on-skill-development-in-india---where-are-we-on-skills

34. Evin M. Tas (2011), ICT education for development – a case study; Procedia Computer Science 3 (2011) 507–512, Doi: 10.1016/j.procs.2010.12.085

35. EY, FICCI, NASSCOM (2017), Future of Jobs in India- A 2022 perspective, https://www.ey.com/Publication/vwLUAssets/ey-future-of-jobs-in-india/%24FILE/ey-future-of-jobs-in-india.pdf

36. FICCI, (2010), The Skill Development Landscape in India and Implementing Quality Skills Training, New Delhi: Federation of Indian Chambers of Commerce and Industry.

37. Fisher, R. A. (1925), Statistical methods for research workers. Edinburgh: Oliver and Boyd.

38. Ganesh, U. (2017). A new paradigm in employability. *NHRD Network Journal, 2*(4), 21-24.

39. Gooptu, N. (2018). JSAD Special Issue on Skill Development in India https://scholar.google.co.in /scholar?q=40.+Gooptu,+N.+(2018).+JSAD+Special+Issue+on+Skill+Development+in+India&hl=en&as_sdt=0&as_vis=1&oi=scholart

40. Grant Thornton, Skilling Ecosystem in India (2020) https://www.grantthornton.in/globalassets/1.-member-firms/india/assets/pdfs/skilling-ecosystem-in-india-unlocking-the-potential-of-youth.pdf

41. Gupta D and Agarwal S (2018), Training Prospects in Power Sector in India, *International Journal of Research in Engineering, IT and Social Sciences*, 08, Special Issue, 305-314.

42. Hajela, R. (2012). Shortage of skilled workers: A paradox of the Indian economy. SKOPE Research Paper No. 111 COMPAS, University of Oxford

43. Hassan Bello, BabawuroShu"aibu (2013), ICT Skills for Technical and Vocational Education Graduates" Employability; World Applied Sciences Journal 23 (2), 204-207, DOI: 10.5829/idosi.wasj.2013.23.02.588

44. Hazarika, S. (2016). Skill Development for Rural Entrepreneurship: A study on State Institute of Rural Development (SIRD), Assam, 3(3), 61–66.

45. Holtzman, S., &Leich, C. M. (Eds.). (2014). *Wittgenstein: to follow a rule*, 4. Routledge.

46. http://www.pmkvyofficial.org/Dashboard.aspx accessed on 28th Feb 2021

47. http://www3.weforum.org/docs/WEF_Future_of_Jobs_2020.pdf accessed on 1st April 2021

48. https://nsdcindia.org/sites/default/files/files/NSDC-Annual-Report-2019-20.pdf

49. https://skillsip.nsdcindia.org/sites/default/files/kps-document/PMKVY%202.0%20Impact%20Evaluation%20Report%20%E2%80%93%20Executive%20Summary.pdf

50. https://wheebox.com/assets/pdf/ISR_Report_2020.pdfaccessed on 15th Jan 2021

51. https://wheebox.com/assets/pdf/ISR_Report_2021.pdf accessed on 15th April 2021

52. https://www.amazon.in/Skill-Development-India-Dr-Ramaswamy/dp/935322280X/refaccessed on 15th April 2021

53. https://www.business-standard.com/article/politics/govt-s-aim-to-skill-10-million-youth-by-2020-falling-64-short-of-target-119020300564_1.html

54. https://www.grantthornton.in/globalassets/1.-member-firms/india/assets/pdfs/skilling-ecosystem-in-india-unlocking-the-potential-of-youth.pdfaccessed on 20th March 2021

55. https://www.mckinsey.com/~/media/McKinsey/Featured%20Insights/Employment%20and%20Growth/A%20new%20emphasis%20on%20gainful%20employment%20in%20India/Indias-labour-market-A-new-emphasis-on-gainful-employment.ashx

56. Hyland, T., & Winch, C. (2007). *A guide to vocational education and training*. Continuum International Publishing Group.

57. IBEF (2013), Skill Development Initiatives and measures in India-A study Report, www.ibef.org/download/skilling-the-workforce.pdf

58. Ian KarmilaYusri and Robert Goodwin (2013), Mobile Learning for ICT Training: Enhancing ICT Skill of Teachers in Indonesia; International Journal of e-Education, eBusiness, e-Management and e-Learning, 3(4), 293–296 DOI: 10.7763/IJEEEE. 2013.V3.243, India. Ministry of Skill Development and Entrepreneurship. (2015). National policy for skill development and entrepreneurship, 2015.

59. International Training Organisation (2010), A Skilled Workforce for Strong, Sustainable and Balanced Growth: A G20 Training Strategy, https://www.ilo.org/skills/pubs/WCMS_151966/lang--en/index.htm

60. Janardhanan, Niranjan S., Mehta, Nimesh. Sinha, Ruchi, (2012). Bridging the skill gap: Opportunities for skills training in India's organized retail sector, GSEI (Global Strategies for an Emergent India) conference, 460-467

61. Kaleb Kelemu, T. Z. P. (2015), Understanding How Rural Youth Learn Knowledge and Skills for Improved Livelihoods: Comparing Case Studies of Mixed Farming and Pastoralist Communities in Ethiopia. Learning for Sustainable Futures Making the Connections. University of Oxford, U.K.

62. Kanchan, S., &Varshney, S. (2015). Skill development initiatives and strategies. *Asian Journal of Management Research*, 5(4), 666-672.

63. Kaptan, S. S., (2014). skill development and capacity building - Role of educational institutions. *Indian Journal of Commerce & Management Studies*, 2, 82-84. Retrieved February 24, 2018, from http://scholarshub.net/ijcms/vol5/issue2/Paper_10.pdf

64. Kapur R, (2014). Skill development In India, International *Journal of Transformations in Business Management,* http://www.ijtbm.com (IJTBM), 4(II)

65. Karnik, Madhura (2016), Even $3 billion may not be enough to solve India's skills crisis, https://qz.com/india/731789/even-3-billion-may-not-be-enough-to-solve-indias-skills-crisis

66. Kataria, Sanjiv (2018), How India can enhance employability of its jobless youth, https://economictimes.indiatimes.com/jobs/

how-india-can-enhance-employability-for-young-indians/
articleshow/66650380.cms

67. Katole, H. (2015). Skill development and Economic growth of India. Pune University, Pune. Retrieved from http://www.aebjournal.org/articles/0304/030401.pdf.

68. Kaur, A. (2020). From skills to work and aspirations: An examination of Barefoot College and Prime Minister's Skill Development Programmes in India (Doctoral dissertation, University of Cambridge).

69. Kaushik, K. (2014). Vocational Education in India. *International journal of education and information studies*, 4(1), 55-58.

70. Kedar, M.S. (2015). Skill Development in India Challenges and Opportunity. *International Research Journal of Multidisciplinary Studies* 1(5). Retrieved from www.irjms.in

71. Kothari, C. R. (2004). Research methodology: Methods and techniques. New Age International.

72. Luck, D.J. and Rubin, R.S. (1987). Marketing Research. Prentice-Hall, Inc.

73. Lussier, R. N., &Achua, C. F. (2015). *Leadership: Theory, application, & skill development*. Cengage learning.

74. Majumdar, R. (1991). Marketing Research Text, Applications and Case Studies. New Age International.

75. Majumdar, S. (2008). Industry-institute interaction to public-private partnership: A journey to excellence. In *International Symposium on Public-Private Partnership in TVET-Challenges, Opportunities and Best Practices, Manila*, 1-11.

76. Malhotra, N. K., Nunan, D., & Birks, D. F. (2017). *Marketing research: An applied approach*. Pearson Education Limited.

77. Malhotra, N. K. (2004). *Review of Marketing Research*. ME Sharpe.

78. Malhotra, N. K. (2015). *Essentials of marketing research: A hands-on orientation*. Essex: Pearson.

79. Mallapur, Chaitanya (2019), Budget 2019 Must Tackle Missed Skill Development Targets Even as Ministry's Funds Go Unutilized,

https://www.indiaspend.com/budget-2019-must-tackle-missed-skill-development-targets-even-as-ministrys-funds-go-unutilised/

80. Mallick, Anindya (2015), Perspectives Skill India, https://www2.deloitte.com/in/en/pages/tax/articles/skill-india.html

81. Mariama Deen-Swarray, MphoMoyo and Christoph Stork (2013); ICT access and usage among informal businesses in Africa; 15(5), 52-68, Emerald Group Publishing Limited, DOI 10.1108/info-05-2013-0025

82. Matthews, P. (2007). ICT assimilation and SME expansion. *Journal of International Development: The Journal of the Development Studies Association*, *19*(6), 817-827.

83. Mbeki, S. (2014). Causes, effects and impact of shortages of skilled artisans on contractor productivity. http://etd.cput.ac.za/handle/20.500.1

84. Mehdi, A., & Chaudhry, D. (2015). Human capital potential of India's future workforce.

85. Mehrotra, S. (2016). Bridging the Skill Gap. The Hindu, August 3, 2016. Available at: http://www. thehindu.com/opinion/op-ed/Bridging-theskill-gap/article14547715.ece

86. Mehrotra, S. (2009). The international market for public policies on skill development: the special case of India, Planning Commission, Government of India, Paper prepared for the NORRAG Conference on Policy transfer or Policy Learning: Interactions between International and National Skill Development Approaches for Policy Making.

87. Mehrotra, S. (2020). The National Skills Qualification Framework in India: The Promise and the Reality, Available at https://think-asia.org/handle/11540/11860

88. Mehrotra, Santosh, Gandhi, Ankita, Sahoo, Bimal K. (2013). Estimating the Skill Gap on a Realistic Basis for 2022, Institute of Applied Manpower Research Planning Commission, Government of India, https://www.researchgate.net/publication/295598089_Estimating_India's_skill_gap_on_a_ ealistic_basis_for_2022

89. Mehrotra, V. S. (2016). Nveqf: skill development under the national skills qualifications framework in India: imperatives and challenges. In *India: Preparation for the world of work*, 281-310. Springer VS, Wiesbaden.

90. Middleton, J. (1993). *Skills for Productivity: Vocational Education and Training in Developing Countries.* Oxford University Press, 200 Madison Avenue, New York, NY

91. Ministry of Skill Development & Entrepreneurship (2015). National Skill Development Mission, a framework for implementation; https://www.msde.gov.in/nationalskillmission.html,1-32

92. Ministry of Skill Development & Entrepreneurship (2019). Initiatives to improve quality of Skills for better employment opportunities, http://pib.nic.in/PressReleaseIframePage.aspx?PRID=1562827

93. Ministry of Skill Development and Entrepreneurship (2018), Skill India- Highlights 2018, http://pib.nic.in/PressReleseDetail.aspx?PRID=1515326

94. Ministry of Skill Development and Entrepreneurship (2018). Year End Review, 2017, https://pib.gov.in/PressReleasePage.aspx?PRID=1515326

95. Ministry of Skill Development and Entrepreneurship (2021). Status of Skilled Youths in India, https://pib.gov.in/PressReleasePage.aspx?PRID=1697809

96. Misra, S. K. (2015). Skill Development: A Way to Leverage the Demographic Dividend in India, *GSTF Journal on Business Review* (GBR), 4(2), DOI 10.7603/s40706-015-0019-0 20.

97. Mohan, S. (2017). Indian policy and development. McGraw-Hill Education.

98. Mohanraj, P. (2013). Changing scenario of unorganised sectors in India: An empirical study. Facts For You, December 2013, accessed from https://lfymag.com/admin/issuepdf/13-16_Unorganised%20 Sectors%20in%20India_FFY%20Dec%2013.pdf

99. MSDE (2016). Report of the Committee for Rationalization and Optimisation of the Functioning of the Sector Skill Councils, Volume I. Ministry of Skill Development and Entrepreneurship,

Government of India, New Delhi. Available at: http://msde.gov. in/assets/images/ssc-reports/ SSC per cent20Vol per cent20I.pdf

100. MSDE (2017). Annual Report 2016-17. Ministry of Skill Development and Entrepreneurship, Government of India. Available at: http://www. skilldevelopment.gov.in/assets/images/annualpercent20report/ Annualpercent20Reportpercent202016-2017 percent20-percent20 English.pdf

101. MSDE, 2021. Guidelines for Pradhan Mantri Kaushal Vikas Yojana 3.0 (2020-21) https://www.msde.gov.in/sites/default/ files/2021-01/PMKVY%20Guideline%20report_(06-01-2021)_ V5.pdf

102. Nandi, T. K. (2016). Intergenerational persistence of Industry in India. *The European Journal of Development Research*, *28*(3), 495-511.

103. Naresh Malhotra and Satyabhushan Dash. (2013). Future of research in marketing in emerging economies. *Marketing Intelligence & Planning*, 31(2), Available at https://doi.org/10.1108/mip.2013.02031baa.001

104. National Planning Commission. (2013). National development plan vision 2030.

105. National Statistical Commission, Government of India, (2014). Report of the Committee on Unorganised Sector Statistics (February 201), Retrieved from available at http://mospi.nic.in/ mospi_new/upload/nsc_report_un_sec_14

106. NCAER (2018). Skilling India: No Time to Lose, http://www. ncaer.org/event_details.php?EID=243

107. NitiAayog (2015). Report of the Sub Group of Chief Ministers on Skill Development; http://www.niti.gov.in/skill-development, i-viii, 1-227.

108. NSDC (2015). Briefing of Pradhan Mantri Kaushal Vikas Yojana http:// pmkvyofficial.org/App_Documents/News/PMKVY_TPs% 20Meeting_20150514.pdf

109. NSDC (2017). How Skill India is empowering workers to become employable, http://employmentnews.gov.in/NewEmp/ MoreContentNew.aspx?n=WebExclusive&k=58

110. NSDC (2018). Candidates placed under PMKVY, https://www.msde.gov.in/assets/images/latest%20news/PMKVY%20Placement%20release.pdf

111. NSDC (2019), Annual Report 2017-18, https://www.nsdcindia.org/sites/default/files/files/Annual-Report-NSDC-2017-18.pdf

112. NSDC Annual Report (2019), Annual Report 2018-2019, https://nsdcindia.org/sites/default/files/files/NSDC-Annual-Report-2018-19.pdf

113. NSDC (2020), Annual Report 2019-2020 https://nsdcindia.org/sites/default/files/files/NSDC-Annual-Report-2019-20.pdf

114. NSDC (2020). PMKVY 2.0, Impact Evaluation Report, https://skillsip.nsdcindia.org/sites/default/files/kps-document/PMKVY%202.0%20Impact%20Evaluation%20Report%20%E2%80%93%20Executive%20Summary.pdf

115. OECD, I. (2016). Energy and Air Pollution: World Energy Outlook Special Report 2016.

116. Okada, A. (2012.). Skills Development for Youth in India: Challenges and Opportunities. Journal of International Cooperation in Education, 5(2), 169-193. Retrieved February 5, 2019, from http://home.hiroshima-u.ac.jp/~cice/wpcontent/uploads/publications/15-2/15-2-10 .pdf

117. Organisation for Economic Co-operation and Development (OECD) (2015). World Indicators of Skills for Employment (WISE) database, http://www.oecd.org/employment/skills-for-employment-indicators.html

118. Özge Yaşar & Şirin Karadeniz (2011). The power of social media in informal learning, Education in a technological world: communicating current and emerging research and technological efforts; FORMATEX 2011, 531 – 538

119. Panagariya, A. (2007), Why India lags behind China and how it can bridge the gap, The World Economy, 30(2), 229-248.

120. Pandey, A., & Nema, D. K. (2017). Impact of skill India training programme among the youth. *International Journal of Multidisciplinary Research and Development*, 4(7), 294-299.

121. Pandey, S. (2016), Improvising Skill Development & Employability Potential through Higher Education, Research & Innovations in India, International *Journal of Innovative Research in Science, Engineering and Technology*, 5, (1), 2319-8753.

122. Paneerselvam, R. (2004). Research Methodology, Prentice Hall of India.

123. Parihar Suresh Dahake, D., Bansod, S. N., &Dahake, N. S. (2020). 'Skill Development Education Initiatives A Path towards Entrepreneurship and Employment Creation for the Youth. *Psychology and Education Journal*, *57*(9), 1443-1450.

124. Patnaik, B. C. M., Satpathy, I. & Rachayeeta, P. (2016). Issues of micro, small and medium enterprises (MSME) in India. *International Journal of Innovative Research and Development*, *5*(6), 1-5.

125. Patnaik, B. C. M., Satpathy, I., & Suhagin S. (2018), Role of ITeS In Pradhan Mantri Kaushal Vikas Yojana (PMKVY): A Conceptual Study. International Journal of Mechanical Engineering and Technology (IJMET), 9(9), 907–914, Available online at http://www. iaeme.com/ijmet/issues.asp?JType=IJMET&VType=9&IType=9

126. Pearson, M. and Sharma, M. (2011). 'Where are India's skilled workers?' Business Week, 6 January.

127. People Matters (2017). Skill India - What is the impact and what needs to be done? https://www.peoplematters.in/article/ skilling/skill-india-what-is-the-impact-and-what-needs-to-be-done-16659

128. Prasad, J. and Purohit (2017). Skill Development, Employability and Entrepreneurship through Make in India: A Study. *Journal of Engineering Research and Application*, 7(12), 18-28

129. Punia.B.K. (2002). Training Needs identification in Indian Organisations - A study. *Indian Journal of Training and development.* 32 (1), 29-39.

130. PWC, FICCI (2019), Fast Forward- Relevant Skills for Buoyant Indian Economy, https://www.pwc.in/research-insights/2019/ fast-forward.html

131. PWC (2017). Workforce for the future, https://www.pwc.com/gx/en/services/people-organisation/publications/workforce-of-the-future.html

132. Raina, N., (2013). Skilling Initiative for Undergraduate students at the entry level: A Case study. *Journal of Commerce & Management Thought*, 4(4), 843- 853.

133. Raju, S. V., Raju, M. B., Abbaiah, G., &Gudavalli, M. (2016, February). Role of ICT in outcome-based education. In *2016 IEEE 6th International Conference on Advanced Computing (IACC)*, 815-819. IEEE.

134. *Ramaswamy B, PushpaSasikala and Gururaj M.B. (2019). https://www.amazon.in/Skill-Development-India-Dr-Ramaswamy/dp/935322280X/ref*

135. Rani, K. (2021). Role of Pradhan Mantri Kaushal Vikas Yojana in promoting employability skills in Haryana state. *International Journal of Economics, Business and Human Behaviour*, 2(2), https://ijebhb.com/index.php/ijebhb/article/view/19

136. Rashmi Dewangan (2018). Empowering Rural Youth through Pradhan Mantri Kaushal Vikas Yojana (PMKVY), *International Journal of Basic and Applied Research*. 8 (8), 945-951

137. Ravikumar, S. (2018) Skill Development in India-Present Scenario and Challenges. *International Journal of Humanities & Social Science Studies*, 5(1), 27-35

138. Richardson, S., &Teese, R. (2008). A well-skilled future. *Australian Bulletin of Labour*, *34*(2), 125-153.

139. Saleem, Q., Shahid, M., &Naseem, A. (2011). Degree of influence of training and development on employee's behavior. *International journal of computing and business research*, *2*(3), 2229-6166.

140. Sanghi, S., & Srija, A. (2016). Entrepreneurship development in India-the focus on start-ups. *Special Article, Laghu Udyog Samachar, January*, 20-27.

141. Sanghi, Sunita, Parvathy, Lakshmi, Khurana, Sakshi (2018). India needs to Develop Skill Development Indicators, http://niti.gov.in/content/india-needs-develop-skill-development-indicators, Mint, 19th April 2019

142. Sanghi, Sunita and Sirja, A., (2015). Skill Development and Productivity of the Workforce, CII-NITI AAYOG, http://www.niti.gov.in/writereaddata/files/document_publication/Skill%20Development%20and%20Productivity%20of%20the%20Workforce.pdf

143. Saunders, M., Lewis, P. and Thornhill, A. (2009). Research Methods for Business Students, (5th ed), Essex: Pearson Education Limited

144. Sekaran, U. (1983). Methodological and theoretical issues and advancements in cross-cultural research. *Journal of international business studies*, 14(2), 61-73.

145. Selvaraj, D. (2019). "Sankalp"-Innovative skill development in industrial knowledge. *Asian Journal of Multidimensional Research (AJMR)*, 8(7), 108-113.

146. Sharda Prasad (2016), Report of the Committee for rationalisation and optimisation of the functioning of the sector skill councils, https://www.msde.gov.in/assets/images/ssc-reports/SSC%20Vol%20I.pdf

147. Sharma, L., &Nagendra, A. (2016). Skill development in India: Challenges and opportunities. *Indian Journal of Science and Technology*, 9(48), 1-8.

148. Sharma, Ragini (2016), Skill Development- Impact on Economic Growth, http://www.professionalpanorama.in/wp-content/uploads/2016/05/11-Ragini-Sharma.pdf

149. Sharma, S. and Sharma, P. (2017), Educational mismatch and its impact on earnings: evidence from Indian labour market, *International Journal of Social Economics*, 44(12), 1778-1795. https://doi.org/10.1108/IJSE-05-2016-0134

150. Sharma, S. (2016). Entrepreneurship Development. PHI Learning Pvt. Ltd.

151. Shrivastav, R. K. &Jatav, A. (2017). An Analysis of Benefits and Challenges of Skilling India. 9th International conference on science, technology and management, Indian Federation of United Nations Association, New Delhi, Retrieved from http://conferenceworld.in.

152. Shyamsukha, Narendra (2018). Skill development challenges in India and how to overcome them, http://educationtechnology.in/2018/01/12/skill-development-challenges-in-india-and-how-to-overcome-them/

153. Singh, Ashutosh Prasad (2018). Presentation on the Report of Sharda Prasad Committee on Skill India Reforms, http://csdindia.org/wp-content/uploads/2018/07/Dr.-Ashutosh_Skill-India-Reforms.pdf

154. Singh, R., &Mohanty, M. (2012). Impact of Training Practices on Employee Productivity: A Comparative Study, *Inter Science Management Review* (IMR), 2(2), 87-92.

155. Singh, S., & Kaur, K. (2018). A Study on Skill Development of Paint and Coating Industry. *Kurukshetra University, Kurukshetra–Haryana*, 5, 2348-1269.

156. Singh A & Sanjeev R. (2016). Need for re-skill training towards make in India initiative. *Independent Journal of Management & Production*, 7. 1115-1125.

157. Skill India- Kushal Bharat (2019). Skill India: How industry-driven training is improving the employability of our youth, https://yourstory.com/2019/02/skill-india-industry-driven-training

158. Surabhi, Nigam, Aditi (2017). Just about half the candidates who get skilled land jobs, https://www.thehindubusinessline.com/economy/policy/just-about-half-the-candidates-who-get-skilled-land-jobs/article9578024.ece

159. Tara, S. N., & Kumar, N. S. (2016). Skill development in India: In conversation with S. Ramadorai, Chairman, National Skill Development Agency & National Skill Development Corporation; former CEO, MD and Vice Chairman, Tata Consultancy Services. *IIMB Management Review*, 28(4), 235-243.

160. Tara, S. N., & Kumar, N. S. (2016). Skill development in India: In conversation with S. Ramadorai, Chairman, National Skill Development Agency & National Skill Development Corporation; former CEO, MD and Vice Chairman, Tata Consultancy Services. *IIMB Management Review*, *28*(4), 235-243.

161. Tara, S. Nayana, Kumar, N.S. Sanath (2016). Skill Development in India: in Conversation with S. Ramadorai, IIMB Management Review 28, 235–243, https://www.sciencedirect.com/journal/iimb-management-review/vol/28/issue/4

162. Tata Institute of Social Sciences- Axis Bank Foundation (2015), Skill Development Initiatives,http://www.axisbankfoundation.org/download/knowledge-corner/TISS-ABF-Skill-Development-Report.pdf

163. The Wire (2017). How Modi's Flagship Skill India Project Stumbled Hard in Its First Year, https://thewire.in/economy/modi-skill-india-stumbled

164. Tustin, D. H. (2005). Marketing research in practice. Unisa Press.

165. UN (2003) Human Development Index Reveals Development Crises, UNDP Human Development Report. http://hdr.undp.org/reports/

166. UN (2003). The Human Development Report 2003, UNDP Human Development Report. http://hdr.undp.org/reports/

167. UN (2004) The Human Development Report 2004, UNDP Human Development Report. http://hdr.undp.org/reports/

168. UNDP, India Skills Report 2018, https://www.undp.org/content/dam/india/docs/poverty/india-skills-report-2018_undp.pdf

169. UNFPA. (2011). *Impact of demographic change in Thailand*. Bangkok, Thailand: United Nations Population Fund.

170. UNICEF (2012). "Global evaluation of life skills education programmes." *New York: United Nations Children's Fund*

171. United Nations in India, Skilling, Entrepreneurship and Job Creation (2013). http://in.one.un.org/job-creation-skilling-and-entrepreneurship/

172. Varma, Subodh (2018). Modi's Failures: The Skill Development Disaster, https://www.newsclick.in/modis-failures-skill-development-disaster

173. Venkatanarayana, M., &Mahendra Dev, S. (2012). Youth employment and unemployment in India. http://hdl.handle.net/2275/138

174. Vyas, Mahesh (2018). Jobs are human capita; quality of Indian jobs is falling; https://timesofindia.indiatimes.com/blogs/toi-edit-page/jobs-are-human-capital-quality-of-indian-jobs-is-falling-there-are-fewer-rewards-for-getting-an-education-today/

175. Wheebox, People Strong, CII (2015). India Skills Report 2015, https://wheebox.com/logo/India%20Skills%20Report2015.pdf

176. Wheebox, People Strong, CII (2017). India Skill Report 2014, https://wheebox.com/static/wheebox_pdf/india-skills-report-2017.pdf

177. Wheebox, People Strong, CII (2019). India Skills Report/2019 https://www.aicte-india.org/sites/default/files/India%20Skill%20Report-2019.pdf

178. Wheebox, UNDP, CII, AICTE, Association of Indian Universities (2020). India skills Report 2020 https://wheebox.com/assets/pdf/ISR_Report_2020.pdf

179. Wheebox, UNDP, CII, AICTE, Association of Indian Universities, India skills Report (2021) https://wheebox.com/assets/pdf/ISR_Report_2021.pdf

180. Wipro-NASSCOM (2019). Talent and New ways of working in the age of digital transformation, https://www.nasscom.in/knowledge-center/publications/talent-and-new-ways-working-age-digital-transformation

181. Woetzel, Jonathan; Madgavkar, Anu and Gupta, Shishir (2017). India's labour Market, A New Emphasis on Gainful Employment, Mckinsey Global Institute, June 2017, http://center4affordablehousing.org/wp-content/uploads/2019/01/India-labour-market-A-new-emphasis-on-gainful-employment.pdf

182. Woody, C. (1927). The values of educational research to the classroom teacher. *The Journal of Educational Research*, *16*(3), 172-178.

183. World Bank (2017). Skilling India, http://www.worldbank.org/en/news/feature/2017/06/23/skilling-india

184. World Bank Report (2019). The Changing Nature of Work, http://www.worldbank.org/en/publication/wdr2019

185. Yash Pal Sharma (2010)."Skill Development Programmes in India" November 1-12, http://www.bable.in/Knowledge%20Bank

186. Zikmund, W.G. (2000) Business Research Methods. 6th Edition, The Dryden Press, Fort Worth.

187. (https:// www.pmkvyofficial.org / dashboard)